"Whether you're a blushing bride or blowing out the candles on your fiftieth anniversary cake, *The Heart of Marriage* will take you to a new place in your most significant relationship on this earth. The words on these pages will make you laugh, cry, nod your head in understanding, and hold on to the hand of the one you love a little bit tighter today . . . and for a lifetime."

—Holley Gerth, bestselling author of *You're Already Amazing*

"In *The Heart of Marriage*, Dawn Camp has put together an incredible collection of stories that are brimming with love and compassion, challenge and inspiration, humor and passion. Just as marriage is a complex relationship, with layers of mess mixed up with layers of beauty, this book is also a multi-faceted look at a life shared by two people. By featuring stories from writers with varied perspectives and experiences, Dawn has created a meaningful mosaic of marriage that will encourage the heart of every married person, from the honeymoon to their final days."

—Mary Carver, coauthor of *Choose Joy*

"Ecclesiastes 4:12 says that a cord of three strands cannot be quickly broken. In *The Heart of Marriage*, Dawn Camp has gathered story after story of marriages that reflect this truth. It's a wonderfully encouraging book to pick up and read again and again. This one is a keeper!"

—Dee Kasberger, artist, RedLetterWords.com

"There are lots of great books that can teach you how to have a great marriage—the how-to of marriage. But there are not many books that can remind you why working hard to have a great marriage is so vitally important—the motivation behind a great marriage. *The Heart of Marriage* stands apart as a collection of marriage stories that will make you laugh, cry, and remember why you fell in love and got married in the first place. After thirty-plus years of being married and working with countless other married couples, we can wholeheartedly recommend this much-needed book and look forward to *The Heart of Marriage* inspiring couples in their marriage journeys for years to come. Well done!"

—Brad & Tami Miller, TandemMarriage.com

"The best marriage books tell stories because stories penetrate the deep places where rules and regulations cannot go. Dawn Camp has gathered a glorious kaleidoscope of true tales, reminding us that every marriage is unique because every marriage is created between two unique people. This is a book for the newlywed and the one celebrating a hard-earned anniversary. This is a book for the disillusioned and the starry-eyed. The stories in this collection are as varied as the marriages behind them, but together they offer needed wisdom for the always good but sometimes difficult work that is the making of a marriage."

—Christie Purifoy, author of *Roots and Sky*

Books by Dawn Camp

The Beauty of Grace
The Gift of Friendship
The Heart of Marriage

the heart of marriage

STORIES THAT CELEBRATE
THE ADVENTURE OF LIFE TOGETHER

Dawn Camp,
EDITOR AND PHOTOGRAPHER

Revell
a division of Baker Publishing Group
Grand Rapids, Michigan

Published by Revell
a division of Baker Publishing Group
P.O. Box 6287, Grand Rapids, MI 49516-6287
www.revellbooks.com

Printed in the United States of America

Library of Congress Cataloging-in-Publication Data
Names: Camp, Dawn, editor, photographer.
Title: The heart of marriage : stories that celebrate the adventure of life together / Dawn Camp, editor and photographer.
Description: Grand Rapids : Revell, 2017.
Identifiers: LCCN 2016035299 | ISBN 9780800723811 (cloth)
Subjects: LCSH: Marriage—Religious aspects—Christianity.
Classification: LCC BV835 .H444 2017 | DDC 242/.644—dc23
LC record available at https://lccn.loc.gov/2016035299

"The Good Wife: How I (Thought I) Failed My Marriage" by Ann Swindell originally published at TodaysChristianWoman.com.

Published in association with William K. Jensen Literary Agency, 119 Bampton Court, Eugene, Oregon 97404.

17 18 19 20 21 22 23   7 6 5 4 3 2 1

For Bryan, my love,
and for Jacob, Hayden, Christian, Sabra,
Chloe, Clayton, Felicity, and Lily, the fruit of it

contents

foreword

My adorable, almost-twenty-six-year-old medical student was recently home for just a few days. He's been so busy studying and preparing for his board exams that it's rare for us to have time to chat about the good stuff of life. That day, we talked about everything under the sun. Maybe I'm just prejudiced because I'm his momma (almost certainly true), but he's one of my favorite people to spend an afternoon with. He's smart, funny, passionate, and really interested in our advice on important things.

As it often does with twentysomethings, the subject of marriage came up and we all (including my husband) tossed around our ideas about the ideal time to get married these days. Is early marriage better? Should you wait until you have a more stable income? Until you're done with all your schooling? Until your bank account reassures you that you're ready? (That usually never happens, by the way!)

Then my winsome husband, Stevie, piped up, "Well, you just need to decide when you want the real suffering to start, that's all."

Yep, that's what he said. And we all started laughing— me, especially hard. *Because it's true.* And it's so rare that someone will just say it.

I even added, "Yeah, you just have to decide when you're ready to take up your cross, Tay."

And coming off Easter weekend, the metaphors were easy to see.

Yes, of course, there's the really wonderful side of marriage— the sheer joy and love you feel when everything is right and there's no tension and no misunderstanding and no disappointment.

But the part nobody talks about is how hard it all is. The part you're not ready for is the fact that marriage is by far the most daunting thing you'll ever do. Nobody tells you how much sacrifice and forgiveness and dying to yourself there will be. Nobody warns you that the feelings will come and go, that the fire in your belly will peter out and you'll be left with a gnawing sense that maybe it's supposed to be better than this.

And nobody tells you that all of that is normal.

This relationship has been given to us primarily as an instrument of our sanctification and only secondarily as a way for us to find contentment and fulfillment. But we have it backward. We chase after some elusive dream of superficial happiness when no such thing has ever been promised us.

Every Sunday, Stevie and I sit together and publicly confess our sins to each other and to our congregation—that we have not loved God with our whole heart and that we have failed to love our neighbor as ourselves. Without exception, the neighbor I fail the most is him. Always. Every single week.

Why? Because he's the one I can't hide from, the one who sees the best and the worst of me, the one who really knows me and all my stubbornness and sin and frailty.

And then we walk together and kneel at the communion rail, holding out our hands like beggars, believing that this meal will do what Jesus said it would do—bring life and forgiveness and salvation, His very body joining to ours and uniting us both to Him and to each other.

And this is how we finally have peace, when we begin to submit to the sanctifying—dare I say crucifying—work of Christ in our hearts.

The very fact that it feels hard doesn't mean you're failing; it means you're trying, and when you take a closer look you'll see that this very person and this difficult circumstance may be the exact thing God is using to remake you into who He created you to be.

It's hard because it's supposed to be hard. But if you just hold still and stay in the murky mess of it all, a miracle will begin to occur. More likely than not, it'll be the miracle in your own heart that will surprise you the most.

Jesus is the skillful potter, chipping away at our rough edges—our bitterness and hardheartedness and self-righteousness and sin. This is work that hurts us and breaks us and puts to death our ego so that Christ can raise us (and our often flailing marriages) to new life.

C. S. Lewis said it this way:

> Submit to death, death of your ambitions and favorite wishes every day and death of your whole body in the end: submit with every fiber of your being, and you will find eternal life. Keep back nothing. Nothing that you have not given away will ever be really yours. Nothing in you that has not died will ever be raised from the dead. Look for yourself, and you will find in the long run only hatred, loneliness, despair, rage, ruin, and decay. But look for Christ and you will find Him, and with Him everything else thrown in.[1]

Nothing that you have not given away will ever really be yours. Not even your hopes for some polished and perfect fantasy version of marriage.

What I love about this book is that these essays run the gambit. You'll see the beautiful, almost fairy-tale side of marriage and you'll see the hard and gritty side. And we need the peace and comfort from knowing that we're not the only ones with hard, imperfect stories.

Take hope that the real, raw, and gritty version most of us struggle through every day is exactly how it is supposed to be, because it keeps us humble and repentant and all the more thankful when out of nowhere joy sneaks into our everyday mess and overwhelms us. Peace in my marriage finally came when I quit looking for peace with my husband and starting looking for peace with God.

1. C. S. Lewis, *Mere Christianity* (New York: Touchstone, 1996), 190–91.

In a day and age where peace is hard to come by, I'm thankful for Dawn, for her commitment to her own marriage, and for her commitment to seeing marriages supported with true and beautiful words—words that point us to the One we can trust to sustain our marriages and our very lives.

Edie Wadsworth
author, *All the Pretty Things*

acknowledgments

Bryan—The time I've spent contemplating marriage while working on this book makes me love and appreciate you even more. What a perfect place to share our story.

Jacob, Hayden, Christian, Sabra, Chloe, Clayton, Felicity, and Lily—I hope you treasure my and your daddy's love stories that I've written down for you here. I pray your marriages are equally blessed.

My church family—I'm humbled by the many ways you support me and how you love my family so well. You're my favorite people.

Ruth Samsel, my agent—Thank you for your constant advice and encouragement, and for always being a phone call, text, or email away.

My Revell team—You are such a joy to work with. I'm thankful for the opportunities you've given me and the beautiful books we've made together.

My contributors—Thank you to the thirty-eight women and men who shared their stories and made this book possible. The gospel-filled power of your words changes lives.

My Lord, Jesus Christ—You've blessed me with a husband and children beyond anything I could have imagined, and continue to do exceedingly abundantly above all that I ask or think. Thank You for the opportunity to spread Your Word and praise Your name.

introduction

As Bryan and I drove home from dinner and a movie—we both list quality time as our primary love language, so we're a date night waiting for a place to happen—I thought about the love story we witnessed on the screen. Hollywood can craft a good tale and although these were actors (who might not even like each other), what a rich relationship they portrayed. In that moment I had a revelation that for me was revolutionary and I've held on to it for years: as a married woman in a committed relationship, I can have as fulfilling a marriage as anything I see on the screen or read in a novel. It all comes down to what I'm willing to put into it and what I'm willing to ask of my husband. *It's mine for the taking.*

After thirty years of marriage I can tell you that it moves in cycles, some hotter and some cooler, some more connected and some less. How could it be otherwise? But I can also tell you this: what you put into it is directly proportional to what you get out of it. Strive for balance—one spouse shouldn't do all the giving and the other all the taking—but prepare to periodically shift your expectations. Remember your vows? For better or for worse, for richer or for poorer, in sickness and in health. These were penned by someone with an intimate knowledge of the degrees of change, the sometimes delicate and sometimes dramatic shifts of fate and fortune within a healthy marriage.

I remember when Bryan and I realized we'd spent more of our lives married than not. Not only have I been a wife and mother for over half of my life, but we still have a houseful of kids (my mother was an empty nester at my age). Here are some things I've learned from more than thirty years of marriage:

- No matter how wonderful your children are, there will be days when they break your heart; eventually they'll grow up and start families of their own.
- No matter how much you may love your job (if you have one), it's still your work, not your life.
- No matter how supportive your online community may be, they aren't a face-to-face part of your life.
- No matter how close your friends are, they've got their own lives, their own families, and their own obligations.

But your husband—the one you chose and who chose you, till death do you part—*this is the relationship you need to nurture above all others.*

Recently a friend told us about a seminar he attended with his son. The speaker counted down a top-ten list of tips on

17

how to be a better father. When he reached number one, our friend was confused; it was not what he expected. The first nine involved his relationship with his children, but number one? The number-one tip was to love his wife. (If this seminar had been for women, I'm sure the number-one tip would be to love your husband.)

If you have children, a strong marriage is one of the greatest gifts you can give them. It's easy to put their wants and needs above those of your husband, but you can't put your marriage on the back burner for years and expect it to thrive. If our average life expectancy is approximately eighty years and our children live at home for twenty, give or take, you and your husband will live together for forty to sixty years, depending on your age at marriage and other factors. Obviously *this* relationship needs to work long-term. Protect, treasure, and preserve it above all others. Contrary to how easy it is to dissolve this till-death-do-us-part union, marriage was never meant to be disposable.

Kids are smart. They will seek to pit you against each other and divide you as parents because they would rather have one of you on their side than united against them. As they get older and parenting becomes more difficult, you will need your husband's love and support more than you could imagine when your children were young. They need to see the two of you as a unified front and have the security that comes from parents with a stable and loving marriage. When our kids see us hug or steal a kiss they call it awkward, inappropriate, or, the most amusing, a middle-age moment (I have no idea what that means). We not only love each other but we like each other too; it's a gift we give our children every day.

Marriage is a reflection of Christ's relationship with the church and contains specific instructions for both husbands and wives.

> Wives, submit yourselves unto your own husbands, as unto the Lord.
>
> For the husband is the head of the wife, even as Christ is the head of the church: and he is the saviour of the body.
>
> Therefore as the church is subject unto Christ, so let the wives be to their own husbands in every thing.
>
> Husbands, love your wives, even as Christ also loved the church, and gave himself for it;
>
> That he might sanctify and cleanse it with the washing of water by the word,
>
> That he might present it to himself a glorious church, not having spot, or wrinkle, or any such thing; but that it should be holy and without blemish.
>
> So ought men to love their wives as their own bodies. He that loveth his wife loveth himself. (Eph. 5:22–28)

Once the honeymoon is over, you might discover your man has a completely different standard of neatness, body clock, attention to punctuality (don't even get my husband started on this one), social habits, or a host of other personality differences. Not to mention the fact that men and women are just plain different. I'm better at cleaning and my husband is better at straightening. I'm a night owl but my husband needs his sleep to get up early for work. I'm sure my husband doesn't understand my insanely detailed laundry procedures and I still haven't figured out his system of organizing T-shirts or where the tools go. We're different. We may not always understand each other and we may get frustrated, but we love each other and we're on the same team.

After Bryan and I married it was hard to transition from asking my father's opinion to asking my husband's first. Marriage involves more than just two people; it includes their families too. My mother gave me a great piece of advice: don't bad-mouth your husband to your family. You'll kiss and make up, but your family won't forget. I can add to my mother's wise words: if you bad-mouth your husband in front of your kids, you undermine the respect they should have for their father. If it's in front of your girlfriends, they're either going to encourage it, which isn't good for your marriage, or find it uncomfortable, which isn't good for your friendships. No matter how tempting it might be, this is a lose-lose decision. Don't do it. "The heart of her husband doth safely trust in her. . . . She will do him good and not evil all the days of her life" (Prov. 31:11–12).

Two things that can cause a lot of trouble in a marriage are pride and a lack of forgiveness. When these two take root, we magnify our husband's faults without acknowledging our own, we build walls around our heart (or our body) and won't let him in, and we don't say we're sorry (it doesn't matter if he needs to say it too; take responsibility for your own actions). Pride is sneaky; often we don't see it for what it is. I'm not pointing fingers, sisters. I'm guilty too. We sabotage our marriage when we won't tell our husband what we need or make him aware of our expectations (we do this in the bedroom too). We make excuses. *I don't want to seem too demanding. I wouldn't be comfortable saying that. What if he doesn't care?* Men joke about not understanding women because we leave them guessing and they tend to get it wrong. Your husband thinks differently than you. He's not a mind reader and *he probably wants to make you happy.* Help him.

Communication doesn't have to be complicated, and it can be fun when you live in the same house. I picked up a $3.99 wooden block painted with the words "Love You More" at Marshalls, and my husband and I have made a game of leaving it for each other in unexpected places: on top of his car keys, in the clean towel basket, on my essential oils rack, under a pillow, in his underwear drawer (hey, I knew he'd find it!). If you've allowed stubborn pride to set up housekeeping in the middle of your relationship, it's time to call a truce no matter who may be at fault. (There are two sides to every story, amen?) The Lord modeled for us the ultimate act of forgiveness: "As far as the east is from the west, so far hath he removed our transgressions from us" (Ps. 103:12). Leave notes for your husband around the house or in his car, show up at his workplace and take him to lunch—*woo him.* Don't choke on your pride. This is the same man you fell in love with. Tend a spark and you can rekindle the fire.

The book you hold includes stories about marriages of all shapes and sizes. One thing I found again and again as I gathered them: many of these writers experienced dry spells when they weren't sure their marriage would survive. Marriage is a commitment. God commands us to love our spouses, which wouldn't be necessary if it were always easy. Love is more than a feeling; it's an act of the will. Act consistently toward your husband the way you should—even when (or especially when) you don't feel it—and the feelings will come. They will. Your mind is a reflection of your actions. When you do right, you feel right. "Let nothing be done through strife or vainglory; but in lowliness of mind let each esteem others better than themselves" (Phil. 2:3).

Do you believe it? Do you believe marriage can fulfill you the way God intended? Do you believe your love story is being written in both the magic and the mundane moments of your life? That love stories exist beyond the silver screen? That it's yours for the taking?

You may read these words and think they could never apply to you. Your marriage is too broken. Your spouse is too distant. You've built walls between you, and to tell the truth, you're not sure you even care anymore. Or maybe you're content in your marriage but there's no real spark. You coexist peacefully, hardly more than roommates, and no longer remember the flush of attraction that made you choose one another above all others. Or maybe your marriage is great— congratulations!—and these stories will bring a deeper appreciation of what you possess, prepare you to weather future storms, or enable you to empathize with and advise others.

Marriage gets a bad rap in our society, but it provides a framework of love and security where couples can grow and families can thrive, the way God intended. Whether your marriage is in a slump, a stalemate, or a satisfying sizzle, I hope these stories remind you that it's worth fighting for; engender hope that "till death do us part" is possible; and cast a vision that you can survive hard times and emerge stronger, closer, and more in love on the other side. May they open your eyes to the delightful possibilities of life with the man beside you.

So I invite you to grab a cup of tea (and maybe a high-lighter or journal) and settle in as we explore the sweetness, the struggle, the friendship, the fun, the sanctity, the security, the redemption, the romance, the heat, and the very *heart* of marriage.

with this ring

{part 1}

dawn camp

*M*ost people would say my husband and I married too young. Sometimes it made life hard, but I've learned the best things seldom come easy. If hindsight is 20/20, then the Lord brought us together in His perfect timing. Whether eighteen or eighty, my heart would know this man.

We were young and in love and got married in a small New England college town eighteen hundred miles from home, with friends and roommates in attendance, a college newspaper photographer taking pictures, and a justice of the peace officiating. My husband heard David Bowie sing "[get] me to the church on time" on his way to meet me.

I spent all the money in my checking account on a dress off the rack—I'm not sure why Lanz made a dress fit for a bride that year, but I'm thankful they did—and then, determined to pay for my young man's wedding ring myself, I put it on layaway in a small, local jewelry store. Bryan slipped a matching gold band on my finger the day we said I do, but I couldn't pay his off until after our wedding day.

As two Southerners living in New Hampshire, we experienced daily culture shock. And the weather? We'd never seen snow drifts piled to the top of stop signs after the plows cleared the roads. Heck, I'm not sure we'd ever seen snow plows.

We were thankful to make it home to the safety and warmth of our little apartment on the day of our first snowstorm as Southern transplants. We lived on the third floor of a nearly vacant and not-so-glamorous building in a new apartment complex the locals thought looked like army barracks. Our heat came from radiators (another new experience). Bryan took off his gloves, and that's when he noticed his missing wedding ring. Mentally retracing his steps, he realized it must have slipped off as he scraped snow from our windshield before the drive home from work and school.

We worried as we drove back to that small parking lot tucked behind buildings off Main Street. Would we make it there and back as the storm escalated? Would we find the ring? We had to try, especially since we had learned the plows would sweep the snow-covered lot clean first thing in the morning. In a desperate race against the clock, we borrowed a metal detector, used to locate tombstones under the snow in winter, from a funeral home.

We scanned the parking space over and over with the metal detector in that dimly lit parking lot for over an hour and located nothing more than a manhole cover. And then we found it: a single gold band buried in a snowstorm.

If that's not God, I don't know what is.

To be continued . . .

to have
and to hold

To have and to hold, from this day forward . . .
Traditional Wedding Vows

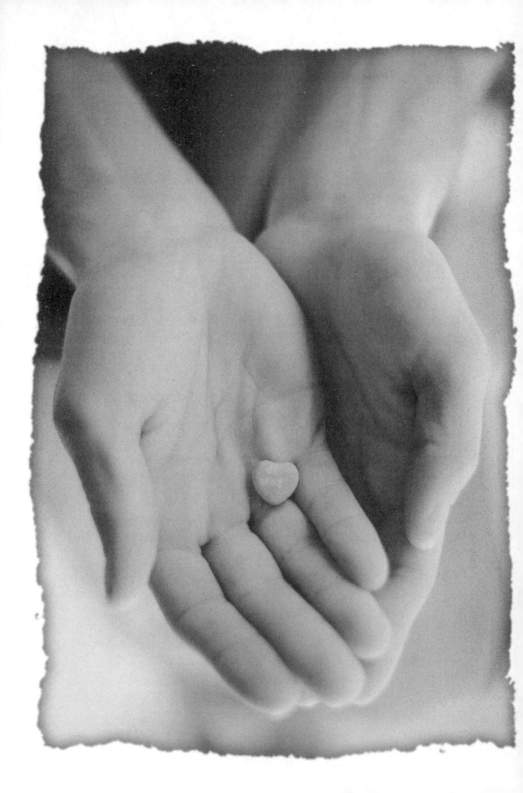

that kiss

shannon lowe

We had a very big wedding, and there were a mind-numbing number of details. I spent the better part of six months making sure it would all go off flawlessly. I was stressed-out and jumpy, and I was a control freak to such a degree that it's remarkable Hubs still married me.

On my list of Wedding Details That Needed To Be Managed was "the kiss." The *you-may-kiss-the-bride* kiss. I suggested to Hubs that we should rehearse it. We had plenty of kissing experience, goodness knows, but this was a very important kiss. What if we clocked each other in the nose in front of four-hundred-plus people? What if, out of nervousness, the kiss was passionless and dull? What if I started laughing?

Hubs had the nerve to say no. We wouldn't rehearse. We'd kiss plenty, and every now and then I'd say, "So, will it be like *that*?" But he would just smile and shrug, much to my dismay, and my pleas fell on deaf ears. I started to worry he had some lovey-dovey mischief up his sleeve, and I reminded him that my dad would be sitting in the second row.

Still, he just grinned. "It'll be a good kiss," he promised. Even then, that man knew how to mess with me.

On our wedding day, things were perfect. Despite my preoccupation with the details, I managed to stay quite focused during the ceremony. I wasn't nervous at all. Until our pastor said, "I now pronounce you husband and wife. You may kiss the bride."

I had exactly .7 seconds to think half of a nervous thought. *Because then he kissed me.*

That kiss, my friends, was The Kiss To End All Kisses. While the specific details of it are meant for my memories only, I'll tell you that I didn't just feel that kiss on my lips. I felt it inside my brain, the very brain that had tried (unsuccessfully) to talk me out of falling in love with this man so quickly. I felt it inside the belly that would someday carry our four as-yet-unknown-and-unplanned-for babies. It traveled all the way down to my feet, the feet that would happily follow this man from the small town to the big city and everywhere in between.

It was a *good* kiss.

And, thankfully, Hubs didn't pack that kiss away with the box of wedding keepsakes that sits in our attic. Every now and then, it reappears. He'll walk in the door from work, usually on a day when my hair is greasy and the kids are fighting and dinner is burning, and he'll plant that same kiss right back on me. My knees go just as weak as they did thirteen years ago.

It's *still* a good kiss.

The sound of a kiss is not so loud as that of a cannon, but its echo lasts a great deal longer.

Oliver Wendell Holmes Sr., *The Professor at the Breakfast-Table*

one simple way
to start a small blaze
in your marriage

lisa jacobson

J could hear his footsteps. Unmistakable. Firm, solid feet.
Man steps. Quite different from the quick pattering of
all the little feet I'd heard throughout the day.

Madly chopping and slicing, I never even looked up when
he entered. I felt frantic and stressed, knowing everyone was
so hungry and I was so far behind in my dinner preparations.
My intentions had been good . . . it's just that I hadn't an-
ticipated that broken glass earlier in the afternoon. Nor the
quarrel between the two children that soon followed. All
of this took time. Then that last urgent phone call put me
hopelessly behind schedule.

And that's how he found me, madly chopping and slicing. He came in behind me, slipping his strong arms around my waist and leaned into me.

I should have felt electricity, but mostly I felt annoyance. *Irritation.* He was slowing me down. I could immediately sense his disappointment. Could feel his arms drop. Without missing so much as a chop, I tried to explain as I kept prepping away. Explain about the day and all its stresses and frustrations. How behind I was in . . . well, in just about *everything.* I thought it might help him understand.

He understood, all right. He understood that those carrots took precedence over him. That I was so busy and my tasks so important that I didn't have a minute to acknowledge him. I couldn't be bothered to turn around. But I wanted him to know that it was simply a matter of timing. I just wasn't ready for love at that moment.

Wasn't ready for love? Did that really come from my mouth? From *my heart?*

The man needed his dinner. No doubt. What he needed even more? A warm, welcoming wife. I was so worried about filling his stomach that it seemed I forgot about filling his heart.

But what if . . . what if I'd done it differently? What if I had dropped those carrots, swept the celery aside, turned around, clasped my hands around his neck, and . . . *ummm* . . . leaned back into him. Stopped my whole world and interrupted my hectic schedule and important plans. To love on him. What then? Then he and I could have started a small kitchen fire.

So what does a husband really need? More than dinner. He needs your eyes to light up when he enters the room. He needs to know how thrilled you are that he's home. How your

35

heart leaps because you two are together again. He needs a warm, welcoming wife. So very warm that the two of you alone could start a small kitchen fire.

I don't know the last time you had a bit of a blaze going, but I highly recommend it. No matter what's gone on in your world, or happened in his day, take a few minutes to turn around and lean into him. Welcome him home. Warmly.

Let the wife make her husband glad to come home and let him make her sorry to see him leave.

Martin Luther (attributed)

the four most important words you can say

francie winslow

Last Tuesday brought a snowy morning and school was, yet again, canceled. Wyatt was getting ready for work and came downstairs dressed in his shiny shoes, blue suit, and cuff links. Enough to make me melt.

The children were running around like little tornadoes and I was in my flannels, hair all kinds of crazy, a bit dazed at the prospect of another day inside with three kids under six.

After grabbing some breakfast, Wyatt's voice rang out over the household madness with the general "Love you" that is said in the common way we do every morning, and he walked out the door to begin scraping the ice off his car.

In that moment, watching him walk out and feeling the harsh, cold air rush into our kitchen as he shut the door behind him, I got a flash of reality.

Nothing in this life is permanent. We're not promised tomorrow. All we have is this moment. This may sound morbid, but I often remind myself how I never want to come to the end with regrets. I never want to wish that I had slowed down enough to take in the moments, the scents, the sights of the ones I love. I might have other regrets, but not these. I want to soak up love and pour out love, every chance I get, with the man I love.

I never want to rush so much that I forget to tell the person closest in my life how I really feel about him. To tell him often, in both simple and extravagant ways, how much I really love him.

Life gets busy and we get on a train that just keeps rolling. But there are days when I get this intense urge to jump off the train and close in on a moment to just "be" with the people I love. To resist the rush and the hurried temptation to take for granted the loves in my life. To reach out and grab them, to hold their faces and speak into their eyes, and say, "I REALLY LOVE YOU."

As I saw that blue suit walk out the door, knowing that the roads were icy and the conditions less than safe, I got that familiar "urge." I needed to jump off the train and let him know afresh, right then and there, that I loved him with all my heart. Before he drove away on those icy roads to work, I had to tell him again, face-to-face.

So I slipped my warm boots over my sockless feet and walked into the garage to stand a few feet from his car parked in the driveway. Standing there in my pink and gray flannel pjs, rubbing my arms with my hands to keep warm while he was scraping ice off of his windshield, I watched him. I took him in, head to toe, inside and out. As he leaned far over the windshield and scraped in his blue suit, I stood thanking God for this good gift. This man. This life partner with whom I run and laugh and pray and dream.

And slowly, I said to Wyatt, "I really love you."

He looked up at me from his ice-task and smiled his big smile. Then he took a deep breath and said, "I really love you too."

In that moment, I felt peace. Because the man I love knows I love him. And again I felt the conviction that I never want to miss a chance to affirm my love to the man in my life.

And above all things have fervent love for one another, for "love will cover a multitude of sins."

1 Peter 4:8 NKJV

choosing love

liz sagaser

Can I ask you something personal? How many times have you fallen in love? Once? Twice? One thousand times and counting? A little more than fifteen years into marriage, I've learned that once the newness wears off, love is not a hapless romantic fall *into* love; rather it is a powerful, conscious choice to fall *back* in.

I know what you might be thinking. *Whoa! Stop trampling on the romance, Negative Nelly!* But I'm proud of the choices I've made in my marriage (most of them, anyway) and the lessons I've learned along the way. I remember the shock I felt as a newlywed when I discovered that the man I married—who was a handsome sixteen-year-old boy who could do no wrong when I first laid eyes on him—had the capacity to disappoint me. To perplex me. To annoy me, even. If somebody told us two crazy kids (we were eighteen and twenty at the time) that marriage wasn't all rainbows, sunshine, and romance once you signed the license, we sure weren't listening. We tussled over everything from dishes (who should do them) to bills (how would we pay them) to having children (what do you mean you *might not want them???*). For the record, we've got two now. So I guess you could say we *both* won that battle.

Several months ago I read an article in my hometown newspaper about Thelma Allen, a longtime resident of Williston, North Dakota. Thelma turned 106 years old this past July, and among the details the article shared about her life was that she'd been married. Three times. To the same man. I had to read that paragraph a couple of times to let it sink in. A friend at the nursing home commented on Thelma's speed on the exercise bike a few years earlier at the age of 99, but what stuck with me was that this couple had mended their broken relationship not once but twice. Sure it sounds a little zany, but I love that they chose each other again—and then *again*. Despite their differences, they chose to love.

Talk about keeping at it.

So when my best friend and love of my life—the boy who caught my eye way back when—does the chores wrong (or not at all), pays a bill late, or deals with the children a little differently than I would have, I remember the choice we made back then, and I make the choice to love him still today. And when he cooks dinner, cleans the litter box without being asked (I love this man!), or plans a romantic evening for just the two of us? The choice to fall in love with him all over again is an easy one.

A successful marriage requires falling in love, many times, always with the same person.

Mignon McLaughlin, *Atlantic* (July 1965)

we used to hold hands

marci stevens

Twelve years ago, I was dating this guy Phil. Man, he was hot! He was short and stocky. Thick, thick thighs and big, beefy arms. The kind of arms I just wanted to be wrapped up in. That kind of thick, muscular chest that I knew would always make me feel safe. Phil and I were as thick as thieves. We did everything together. We rode bikes, went out to eat, went shopping, went to the movies, went dancing, visited each other at school or at work—just everything. And talked. We could talk about anything, and we did. We talked about religion, money, kids, our parents, our family, and how we were raised. We would talk about potholes if it came up. We did not always agree but we enjoyed talking to each other nonetheless.

Then, we got married. And no, the story doesn't abruptly change. No dramatic *dun-dun-duuuuun* music here. We still did mostly all of the same things together that we did when we dated. We would even sit on the same side of a restaurant booth so that we could—guess what?—hold hands! Yes, I know. We were in love. So in love. I could not wait to hear his car pull into the driveway as he returned from work. We purchased a chair and a half (that's fancy talk for a big chair with room for two) so that we could sit with each other in the living room while we watched TV. I hated to be away from Phil. My heart was just so connected to that man. He was charming, tenderhearted, compassionate, and so funny! Man, we really made each other laugh all the time.

Fast-forward twelve years. Okay, now you can hum the dramatic music. Because now the story actually changes. *Dun-dun-duuuuun!* Twelve years after we began being together, with three stepchildren and two of our own, I love Phil today more than I ever loved him—ever. Yet we don't ride bikes together and we don't sit on the same side of the booth at restaurants. I almost loathe going to the movies now and you will never catch me busting a move. Yes, things have changed. I grew. He grew. We each found different favorite activities. Of course, throwing kids in the mix surely changed things too. We have a three-month-old and this past weekend we finally made the time to have our first date out without the baby. I got pretty gussied up for the big night out *that ended at 8:30 p.m.* As we were waiting for our pager to go off for our available table, we sat outside to enjoy the cool air and do some people watching. We both had our phones out. Maybe we checked Facebook a few times, maybe we refreshed to see any new emails. Phil was walking me through Instagram for the first time so at that point we were both engrossed in our phones for sure. We had a good laugh sitting out there, talking about how we were positive that there was a person or

45

couple sitting somewhere near us, looking at us and saying, "Those poor people. They will never make it if they can't go on a date without looking at their phones." We laughed because we know what it may have looked like to others, but we also know what it was to us. To us, it was time alone. It was the old Phil and Marci talking about anything, making each other laugh, and enjoying the bond we share that has twelve years of deep roots.

As we sat and ordered our meal, our dinner was not filled with chitchat like it may have been so long ago. There were silent moments where we just ate or looked around. At some point we traded plates to allow the other to enjoy our meal. Maybe we made some idle talk here and there. But I will tell you something. I would not trade this marriage I have now for the old mushy-gushy marriage I had then for anything in the world. Nothing. I love my marriage and I love the man God provided me. I love who he has become and I love who we are together as a couple. I guess when we are just plain too old to talk I will sit on the same side of the booth with him again. We can share our early-bird specials and hold each other's wrinkly hands. But I know I won't look back and wish we got there any other way.

No matter how old you both get, never stop holding hands, never stop dancing, and never stop saying, "I love you."

Darlene Schacht, *Time-Warp Wife* (February 18, 2016)

sunday mornings
in the kitchen

dawn camp

On Sunday mornings Bryan and I rise long before the first child stirs and shuffle our way into the kitchen. I tie an apron around my pajamas; clean the counter and the stovetop; and then pull mixing bowls, pie plates, slow cookers, and measuring cups and spoons from their hiding places. We eat lunch at church on Sundays, and although a wise woman would prepare it in advance, I prefer to play the fool, for Sunday mornings in the kitchen are one of my favorite times of the week.

Sometimes Bryan joins me in the kitchen when he comes home from work, but everyone wants a word with Dad as he transitions from work and commute to home, and he needs time to unload and unwind. Cooking isn't his thing anyway.

Except for Sunday mornings.

He gathers ingredients for me: flour, oil, eggs, pasta, cheese, milk, butter—always plenty of butter—and pours and measures whatever I need. He's the one who watches the clock on Sunday mornings and knows the faster I cook, the earlier we can leave. I know it pains his sweet deacon's soul to have a wife who's the last one ready, but we do enjoy those early mornings.

Although we might not make the same things each week, we stock the pantry for our standby recipes. Bryan's mastered the art of the perfect pot of cheese grits: triple the four-serving recipe and add an extra cup of water, tablespoon of salt, and half a stick of butter. He stretches an arm for the corn syrup on the top shelf, beyond my reach, and brings me nuts from the pantry for my almost-famous pecan pie. I boil pasta for mac 'n' cheese and he shakes the cans of evaporated milk and then punctures their lids on each side with an old-fashioned can opener. We stir the ingredients together in the slow cooker, which cooks on low until we leave home and then at church during the service. My mother's recipe for unbaked oatmeal cookies, which we call blobs, is prepared in one pan on the stovetop, no oven required.

Sometimes we listen to an audiobook; occasionally we talk current events or politics (he brings me up to speed), but mostly we enjoy this quiet time together as a couple, working in sync, until Bryan notices the time and sends me to the shower and goes to wake the kids. Then chaos ensues. (Lionel Richie wasn't talking about a large family getting ready for church when he sang "easy like Sunday morning.")

We still hold hands during church, and Sunday nights are date nights. Our mornings in the kitchen, gliding past each other in a slow dance between counter, oven, fridge, and sink, contribute to a marital harmony that can be harder to find the rest of the week, when work and schedules fight to keep us apart. So I'll continue to hold on to my sleepy-eyed Sunday mornings in the kitchen and my good man who meets me there.

Cooking is like love: It should be entered into with abandon or not at all.

Harriet van Horne, "Not for Jiffy Cooks"

49

marriage is a sacrament, they say

shawn smucker

When December days are warmer
than they should be, and no one is home,
everyone scattered like dust in different corners
of this city, I sit on the porch and wait
for you.

Arriving without any
of our five children (God bless my mother),
you lead me hand-in-hand into the empty house
that now feels more like a church, a holy space
made up of diagonal light and quiet.

Marriage is a sacrament, they say, a sign
of the sacred.

Outside the house, cars roll down James
Street. Outside the house, people leave the barber's
smelling of aftershave, the wind pulling at
their new hair. Outside the house, December takes
the last leaf from the ancient sycamore. Is there

anything outside the house that knows
of the holy space between us? The way diagonal
light gently rests on rounded sheets? Or
how, later, you hold my hand and we slip inside
a merciful sleep?

Marriage is a sacrament, they say, a sign
of the sacred.

But from the beginning of the creation God made them
male and female. For this cause shall a man leave his
father and mother, and cleave to his wife; And they
twain shall be one flesh: so then they are no more twain,
but one flesh.

Mark 10:6–8

through the eyes of love

For she had eyes and chose me.
William Shakespeare, *Othello*

when i stopped looking through my husband

erin mohring

I'm quite convinced this is not an abnormal scene in America:

A husband arrives home from work to a wife making dinner, kids clamoring for his attention, lots of life and energy and chaos as happens in a home with children. The husband greets everyone and arrives at his wife, working in the kitchen, hoping to kiss her hello, only to receive a quick peck followed by, "I really have to get back to work on dinner. Can you take out the trash? And little Suzy needs to talk to you about what she did today . . ."

Except for the whole "Suzy" thing (and only because I don't have a girl), this has been me far more often than I would care to admit. The arrival of my husband home from

55

work isn't always at the most convenient time, and it opens up a floodgate in me for unloading the day onto him—an adult who will surely understand all the frustrations borne and to-dos left to complete.

Well, go figure that this kind of greeting is not really what my husband or *any human being* would want to experience after a day of their own challenges and tasks. There is no love or warmth or safety of home conveyed in this "welcome." I believe I've found the root cause of this problematic situation that dashes intimacy and creates tension at the very time the family should be coming together.

For far too long, I have been looking *through* my husband. His arrival was briefly acknowledged, but being the person I am, my mind was quickly overcome with the long list of things that still needed to be done *right now*. Instead of really seeing him, I moved to looking through him in order to accomplish the agenda of the household for the rest of the night.

This looking through him instead of at him has made me miss so much. When God opened my eyes to this revelation several months ago, my heart broke because my view of my husband had become so one-dimensional, when in all reality he is a complex, amazing gift whom God gave me to become one with. Here's what I was missing . . .

His Physical Appearance

My husband is a hottie. I've always thought so, but my appreciation for his good looks had dwindled because I wasn't taking the time to really look at him—when we talked, when we ate, when he played with the kids. My lack of appreciation was especially ridiculous because in the past two years he has worked hard to become physically fit and healthy, and he looks better than he ever has before. Making the decision to really linger when looking at him in any situation has greatly amplified my physical attraction to him. And I also mention it to him more often, now that I am more aware! He's a "words of affirmation" guy, so he likes that!

The Ways He Helps Me

My never-ending to-do list was overwhelming me, so when I looked through my husband I completely missed the countless ways he was blessing me. I find myself much more grateful for his help around the house and with finding time for me to write and work out, and for so much more, when I look at him. I knew before that I wouldn't want to live without him, but I'm discovering more and more each day how rich my life is because of his loving, caring ways.

His God-Given Intellect, Talents, and Abilities

When you are looking through a person, you are also probably not hearing them very well. Your mind is elsewhere, and listening intently goes out the window. I have rediscovered how much I love talking about things with my husband, especially things he is passionate and knowledgeable about. We share many interests so those are great fun to discuss, but I even love talking about his work with him because I enjoy his passion for it and the fact God has clearly put his unique skills and talents to great use in his profession. We can go out to dinner and talk for hours, and it is just the most wonderful thing to have this connection.

We celebrated ten years of marriage last May. We have three cute and chaotic boys keeping us very busy. We've been through mountains and valleys together. I feel like this revelation—this looking at him, not through him—is proving to be one of the most important things God has taught me to strengthen our marriage in the everyday.

I encourage you today to really look at your husband— enjoy all of him, appreciate all of him, acknowledge all of him, thank God for all of him. May we be more like the young woman of Song of Solomon, who savors and appreciates every aspect of her lover. And watch God bring new joy to your marriage!

You are so handsome, my love, pleasing beyond words!

Song of Solomon 1:16 NLT

sometimes love in marriage comes down to the smallest of things

lisa jacobson

How can one jar of peanut butter cause so much trouble? No kidding, that's what I wanted to know too. Because apparently it was A Big Problem and he made that quite clear.

My husband was fed up with the sticky, slimy mess dripping down the sides of the peanut butter jar and insisted we put a stop to the madness. "Why can't we keep this jar clean?! There's no reason we should live like this and it's driving me nuts!" He didn't yell, but I could tell by his tone that he really meant it.

Oh, but there was a very good reason, as far as I was concerned, and I protested against his somewhat ridiculous request. Actually, there were *eight* good reasons. You see, we have these things called *children* and one mother can't be on top of everything! Why be so unreasonable? So demanding?

Now, on his behalf, I have to tell you that my husband is not a complainer. He doesn't make negative remarks about my cooking. He doesn't complain about having to throw on his robe in the morning and search for essential items in the laundry room (*Oops! Meant to fold and put those away . . .*). He's even good about patiently sitting in the car and waiting for me to get out the door. And that can be a pretty long wait, sometimes. But the goopy peanut butter container? That just about does him in.

So how many of you moms can I count on to side with me on this one? I mean, we have a bunch of kids and they all make their own peanut butter sandwiches. Even the three young boys. Let's face it—it's a sticky, slimy world we live in. And I basically communicated to him . . . . *Sorry. But that's just the way it has to be.* That we were going to have to learn to live with it. That he was asking the impossible. And I left him in the kitchen, feeling quite justified in my defensive and huffy response. Except for one thing . . .

Epiphany in the Parlor

I left the kitchen to recover and regroup in our front sitting room—our "parlor" as we call it and my very favorite room in the house. *It's a special place.* The parlor has pretty pillows, a tea tray, and a clear glass (*yes, glass*) coffee table.

The kids are not allowed to eat in this room. Or have their electronic gadgets. No LEGOs, dirty socks, or Rollerblades are permitted in the parlor. *Happy sigh.* I love this room.

Now wait! Are you beginning to wonder how it is that I can keep an entire room looking pristine even though we have all these children? With a glass coffee table, no less? Well. It's because it's important to me, of course. *Really important.* But I can't keep the peanut butter jar wiped down?

Right.

Yeah, that's the question that got to me too. You see, I have this tendency to take my priorities very seriously. And this room is one of those. Not only that, but when the rest of my family do their best to keep it the way I like it? It makes me happy. I feel respected. Maybe even *loved.*

I know. It's a small thing. So maybe you don't see why it's a big deal to me. But it kind of is. If at all possible. So, maybe I don't understand all the fuss over the sloppy peanut butter jar. But if it's important to him? Makes him happy? Feel respected? Maybe even *loved . . . ?*

Then I can do this small thing. In fact, I'm determined to have the cleanest peanut butter jar in town.

And if you ever find yourself anywhere near our area, I hope you'll stop by, 'cause I'd love to make you a peanut butter sandwich. Or have that youngest son of ours make you one. He makes the best. It's true that you might have to step over a heaping pile of Rollerblades on the front porch and overlook the baskets of clean laundry waiting to be folded in the living room.

But there should be a nice place for you to sit in the parlor. And you'll be sure to admire the amazingly spotless peanut

61

butter container, won't you? Because he sure does. He likes it that way. But better than that?

He loves *me*.

———

Let each of you look not only to his own interests, but also to the interests of others.

Philippians 2:4 ESV

a secret to marriage for life

robin dance

At seventy-five, he and his bride still hold hands. At times I've seen them look at each other with grins telling secrets, eyes sizzling. Their son ignored it because—gross—but I thought it was amazing.

Marriage is a hard thing, and untended, it will cool.

I want heat.

Even the most blistering of fires will eventually dwindle to ash if not fed.

Give me flames.

He reminded me of the secret to their fifty-four-year marriage, lest there was any doubt, to make certain I understood.

"People want to know how we're still so in love, how we have such a good marriage," he began. And the next thing he said was the kind of thing that pulls your attention taut. "Having a good marriage doesn't have anything to do with trying to have a good marriage."

He would tell you that since his Damascus Road–style conversion in 1970, he has believed and lived out his life verse, Matthew 6:33:

> But seek first the kingdom of God and his righteousness, and all these things will be added to you. (ESV)

So simple. Not easy.

The entirety of his life has been ordered around these words spoken by Jesus. They have shaped how he parents, they have compelled him to minister within prison walls, and they have taught him how to cherish the love of his life.

If you're like me, you're acquainted with family or friends in marital crisis. Maybe you are in crisis, drifting so far apart you've lost hope for recovery. Too much has been said, too much has been done. You've passed the thresholds of anger and pain and settled into a kind of numbness you didn't know was possible. You question whether you were ever really in love with each other.

Let's just sit here a moment and breathe.

I'm praying for you right now, I promise I am. I care because God cares. During a season of depression, I walked in shoes of disillusion and despair, and though my circumstances weren't quite dire, my eyes were opened to an understanding that frightened me, the redemption of which softened my spirit to the hurting in marriage. That dark season in my head and heart gave way to an empathy I couldn't otherwise extend.

Or maybe all of this is foreign, and you think, *I'll never feel like that.* You're still in the newlywed phase when butterflies stampede as he walks in the door. You can't imagine you'll ever grow apart or the quirks you once loved you'll one day despise.

Seek first.

Seek. First.

Think of a triangle where Jesus is at the top and the lines descending from that point represent you and your spouse. You're widest apart at the bottom of the triangle, but as you creep up the sides toward the top—toward Christ—you grow closer together. That image was shared with me ages ago, and it's what I visualized when my father-in-law spoke of Matthew 6:33 as it relates to marriage.

At the genesis of creation, marriage was born in Eden. Sacred and holy, marriage is a lavish gift from God.

Satan has been trying to destroy it ever since.

When invited to share my counsel and thoughts about difficult seasons in marriage, I offer what I know to be true. Mountains have erupted in my life, and I've learned there's a way to the other side.

Sometimes love is spelled c-o-m-m-i-t-m-e-n-t, and barring abuse or ongoing, unrepentant infidelity, honoring the covenant we entered in marriage is best. I realize we can't control our spouse but we can control our own actions . . . and if our heart and behavior is Matthew 6:33-ing, well, it changes how we think, behave, and react.

I tell my father-in-law I'm writing about marriage and I might be quoting him, and he's quick to caution. "Be careful. I don't have all the answers."

And I feel the weight of his words, because I know I don't have half the answers he has. And then I remember something

he wrote—this cowboy-preacher-father-in-love of mine—
twenty-five years ago:

> The essence of love is like fruit on the vine
> It reaches perfection with the passage of time.
> In infancy it flourishes brazen and bold
> but is only perfected as our lifetimes unfold
> Through paths that are narrow and times that are
>   hard
> it's shed abroad in our hearts through the spirit of
>   God
> Without it we fall which we nigh can afford.
> But the essence of love comes only from the Lord.
> So be careful to seek Him while He still can be found,
> and the essence of love in your life will abound.
> What is this essence so precious and true?
> It's the presence of Jesus
> in me and in you.
>
> Tom Dance, October 14, 1989,
> a wedding gift to his second son and bride

He may not have all the answers, but he's got the one that
matters most.

A successful marriage isn't the union of two perfect
people. It's that of two imperfect people who have
learned the value of forgiveness and grace.

Darlene Schacht, *Time-Warp Wife* (October 4, 2013)

the day i said "oh yeah!"

holley gerth

I wore a white dress. He wore a tux. The minister asked me if I would take this man as my husband . . .

And I said, "Oh yeah!" instead of "I do."

Twelve years later it still seems like the right response. Do I know God brought us together? *Oh yeah.*

Has marriage been both more wonderful and difficult (mostly because of me) than I could have imagined? *Oh yeah.*

Am I looking forward to the next twelve years? *Oh yeah.*

Mark and I have been through a lot—so much laughter, our share of tears, holidays and everydays, bike rides and trips, births and deaths, and lots of baked goods (my love language). He's a good man who keeps his feet on the ground so I can have my head in the clouds. I'm glad I said yes in my own way that day.

Yes to whatever came. Yes to what God had planned. Yes to the unknown.

I think that's the way we're meant to live. *Not just saying "I do" with our will but saying yes with our hearts.* With all we are. And all we're yet to be.

A good marriage is where both people feel like they're getting the better end of the deal.

Anne Lamott, *Joe Jones*

what love sounds like

love on purpose

edie wadsworth

Nobody tells you how hard it will be to love someone. Most of us have such a flimsy idea of what love means. You have no idea at the outset of this adventure that this relationship may cost you your life.

The culture has taught us to grab what we need, to get our part, to take care of ourselves. The culture worships at the altar of "me" time. But Christ shows another way.

When our house burned down before Christmas in 2010, Steve and I woke up to a house filled with smoke, with flames shooting out the dining room window. He didn't hesitate. He crawled through the burning house, unlocked the front door, and made a way for our kids to escape.

He didn't count the cost. And as he lay gasping on the front steps, heaving for breath, all he could think about was the kids.

When our sweet daughter Caiti brought them downstairs to safety, she looked like an angel. We all survived by the mercy of God. But for months, I was tortured by the sounds of love—the wheezing, the coughing, the scars that may never heal. The smell of smoke always lingers in the air. He used a steroid inhaler for the longest time, but I'm not sure his lungs will ever be the same.

Every time he coughs, I'm jarred awake to what it means to really love another. Love that will enter a burning room, not knowing the outcome. Love that will lay down its life. Love that will go to work, day in and day out, despite the stress and drudgery and thanklessness.

Love that sets His face like a flint and won't stop until humankind is ransomed. Love that goes to a cross, to die, for the sins of the world.

Real love can't be summed up in chocolate and cards and flowers. Real love is dirty, smoke-stained, bloody, left for dead.

But the Father of all mercy will raise the dead, will give Him breath and life, and will, in His resurrection, raise us too. Love will have the last word.

Love will never fail.

Behold, what manner of love the Father hath bestowed upon us, that we should be called the sons of God.

1 John 3:1

noticing the man in front of me

alexandra kuykendall

I *still remember the days I prayed for the things I have now.*

A spontaneous Friday morning work date. My husband, Derek, sat across from me in a downtown hotel lobby with Wi-Fi and coffee for the taking, our respective laptops open in front of us. When we'd realized we were headed to the same lunch event, we decided to capitalize on the sitter's morning arrival to head downtown together a few hours early to get some work done.

We both had our agendas for the hour, to-do lists to take care of, and emails and phone calls that needed to be checked off. Sitter time is precious work time for me. I can't spend it on conversation that can be covered when I'm not paying someone by the hour. It's my time away from the house to think. So this was a side-by-side date, a "Let's be close to each other while we're working on our own stuff" kind of hour.

In between emails I glanced up from my screen and caught sight of my husband in full conversation on the phone across the table from me, his halfsie reading glasses on, hair gray around his temples. An aged version of the young man I fell in love with nearly twenty years ago. It surprised me to see this older version of my groom. It's not that I don't see him multiple times every day, I do. It's that I often look past him to the dishes on the kitchen counter that need to be washed or the four-year-old who is stuffing multiple pieces of months-old Halloween candy in her cheeks like a squirrel.

The whirlwind of parenthood sidetracks me from the noticing.

Maybe it was the lack of distractions or simply seeing him in full work mode that reminded me we're not twenty anymore. I sometimes see those computer-generated time-lapse photos that show how someone will age, and I wonder if I'd want to know what we both will look like in ten, twenty, thirty years. Would we have wanted to know on our wedding day what we'd look like today? Who we'd be today?

As I looked at the middle-aged man in front of me, I remembered for the gazillionth time that there is no other person I'd rather work with side by side. The years together are victories, some of them hard won, I am both proud of and cherish. So if you see those years on our faces, it's okay. It's more than okay—it is good. Because today we better know who we are and what we're about.

And we've changed. Not just physically, but we've grown into the current versions of ourselves together. He is not the same man I married, nor the same man I was married to a year ago.

73

So today, as I notice my husband in front of me, I am grateful. For what he works on today. For how he parents today. For how he loves me today. Tomorrow I will be married to a different version. A more refined edition of my husband who will be further shaped by life and grace. But I don't want to miss today. Because in many ways today is the answer to my prayers of years ago.

All good is born in [prayer], and all good springs from it.

Charles Spurgeon, *The Spurgeon Series 1855 &*
1856: Unabridged Sermons in Modern Language

how love changes everything

shelly miller

When I enter the bedroom and put my phone on the charger for the night, he lies on my side of the bed, warming up my spot. He has loved me this way for as long as I can remember. And when I approach my side of the bed to crawl in, he looks up from the Kindle to see my eyes and asks, "How are you?"

It's not a casual question. He's looking for the truth. I hesitate to respond. Because sometimes the truth of what we hide on the inside, when self-doubt enters through the back door, isn't pretty. I vacillate. Count the cost of revealing the truth about the lies I have just told myself.

That I feel insignificant when I read about what others do to advance the kingdom, wondering if I do enough. And really, it's not just about sharing my faith; the accusations shout when it comes to parenting and being a wife, a friend, a housekeeper, a writer. Am I enough? Doing enough?

And when I tell him what swirls in my cerebral hemisphere, he throws his hands up in exasperation. Exasperation over my refusal to believe the truth he has told me repeatedly for twenty-one years now. That I am beautiful just the way I am, that God uses me in ways unique to how He created me, that I am *enough*.

Comparison is a sneaky diversion, a fork in the road to destiny. This truth telling, it keeps me from wrong turns, road-blocks, and major delays due to reconstruction. It splits me open to heaven's eyes, puts me back on the journey to hope.

When he apologizes, says he is sorry for the way he responds, love clears the fog that hangs between conviction and condemnation. Clears vision when the reflection of me blurs.

It is hard to explain how love from a man that stands sturdy through wavering days and wondering can transform a girl into a woman. Explain how fragments become pieces of beauty when tended by a farmer of truth who trusts in the power of redemption above sainthood to grow a person.

Marriage isn't about meeting needs but laying them down and forgetting you ever had them.

When I crawl into the warm spot he left on my side of the bed, curl up next to him, hold on to his arm, I laugh. All that guilt I carried into the room, it looks hilarious and out of place lying here beside love.

> Trust in the LORD with all thine heart; and lean not
>   unto thine own understanding.
> In all thy ways acknowledge him, and he shall direct
>   thy paths.
>
> Proverbs 3:5–6

as long as we both shall live

I promise to love and cherish you, to honor and sustain you, in sickness and in health, in poverty and in wealth, in the bad that may darken our days, in the good that may light our way. . . . Beloved, I promise to be true to you in all things until I die.

Francine Rivers, *Redeeming Love*

how to make
a marriage flourish

dawn camp

When the first two of our sons got married this spring (three weeks apart), my husband embraced the father-of-the-groom's job of making a toast at the rehearsal dinner. He put a lot of thought into it, as you should when making a speech in front of your soon-to-be daughter-in-law and her family, who will hopefully still want to merge with your family when you finish. (We've all seen horrifically failed wedding toasts in movies, so I admit I was nervous when he began.)

It's one thing to know your marriage works—and ours does: we celebrate thirty years this fall—but it's another to analyze why and put it in words. It's also interesting to hear why it works from your husband's perspective.

When he raised his glass and toasted the happy couple at the first wedding, here are some of the things my husband said:

1. Always treasure the love you share now and keep trying to impress each other like when you first sought to win each other's affection. (As an aside: I've been known to say "You're still supposed to try to impress me!" when my husband burps loudly or does something else you wouldn't do in front of your future wife in the early stages of the relationship.)

2. Never go to bed mad or angry with each other. (I know this has been said before, and it isn't always easy, but number three should help . . .)

3. Son, odds are she's right. Even if you're not wrong, she's still right. Even when you are right . . . she's still right. Realize this. Accept this. Own this.

4. Finally, always put each other first: each other's needs, wants, and desires. Making your spouse happy will in turn make you happy. That's what they call love, and I know you have it.

Wise words! Admittedly, I saw backs bristle over number three. People are instinctively selfish, and there are philosophies in this world that do not encourage a selfless, put-others-before-yourself attitude. Christianity doesn't happen to be one of them.

Yes, there will be times when my daughter-in-law will be wrong, but I think my son got the message.

Philosophies don't get married, people do, and successful marital relationships aren't governed by political ideologies.

If you're accustomed to interacting with people through a framework of belief systems, it may be difficult to grasp my husband's message: in marriage, harmony matters more than winning.

When we focus on getting our way or having the last word, harmony eludes us. Marriage is a team sport and we only win when we work together. Making your spouse happy should make you happy too (and vice versa).

Ideologies don't make chicken soup when you're sick, hold your hand, or grow old with you. People in loving, harmonious relationships do that. Trust, compromise, and give-and-take when needed.

Following my husband's simple advice—continue to woo one another, don't hold on to anger, you don't have to be right, make your spouse's happiness a priority—can feed a starved relationship and make your marriage flourish the way you both intended the day you said "I do."

Marital fidelity . . . involves the public or institutional as well as the private aspect of marriage. One is married to marriage as well as to one's spouse. But one is married also to something vital of one's own that does not exist before the marriage: one's given word.

Wendell Berry, *The Art of the Commonplace: The Agrarian Essays*

a new perspective

gregory bledsoe, md

Have you ever had a situation where your perception of some event or entity changed dramatically in an instant? I specifically remember an instance of this happening to me while working as a junior medical student in a family practice clinic.

It was a typical day and I was doing the typical thing you're supposed to do as a medical student—feign interest in the clinic's goings-on and try not to get in the way. It had been one patient after another, until eventually we walked into the room of an elderly female patient and her husband.

The patient was close to eighty years old and wheelchair bound. Her limbs were contracted with some neuromuscular disease, and she sat tilted to the side with her mouth agape, drooling. It was a pitiful sight.

What was unusual was the spry energy of her spouse. He was alert, mentally sharp, even loquacious. He was equal to his feeble wife in age but in far better health. I was surprised because so often it is the other way around. We men tend to go downhill much more quickly than women, so usually it's a feeble husband being cared for by his healthy wife.

I must confess, I felt sorry for this husband. Even though he seemed to be in good spirits—and during the course of our visit took care to wipe the drool off his wife's chin so it didn't stain her shirt—I could imagine that it was a difficult situation. His wife obviously needed a lot of care, and by her records I could see she still lived at home with him.

I was preoccupied with this line of thinking when the resident physician I was working with received a page and stepped into the hall to answer it, leaving me sitting alone in the exam room with this patient and her husband. It was a bit awkward.

At this point in my medical training I was basically an observer, so there was nothing I could contribute to the patient's medical care on my own. With my resident out in the hall, the clinic visit had come to a halt, and the patient's husband and I were left sitting together in the presence of his drooling and occasionally moaning wife with nothing more to do than make polite small talk. However, I didn't really know what to say.

I remember formulating in my mind some clichéd phrase to say in an attempt to demonstrate that I recognized the difficulty of his situation. Just as I opened my mouth to speak it, though, his voice broke the awkwardness.

"She's my fishing buddy, you know," he said.

"I'm sorry?" I asked, not really sure what he was getting at.

"She's my fishing buddy. Me and her have fished all over," he said.

"Really?" I asked.

"Yep. We used to set trout lines in the lake over there and get up every morning to check them," he replied. "We've been married over fifty years."

I stared at this man.

His eyes were sparkling, his mouth wide in a jovial, somewhat toothless grin.

He was beaming.

"Yes, sir, this one here's my fishing buddy," he said again, as he gently took her hand and affectionately smiled in her direction.

For the next ten minutes I was transfixed as this man, who moments before I had pitied, regaled me with story after story of his life together with his wife. It was incredible. What was even more incredible, however, was the change that occurred in me.

Watching this elderly man caress his wife's hand, kiss her cheek, wipe away her drool, and joyfully recount their lives together provoked a powerful transformation of perspective within me. Gone was any semblance of pity.

Instead, in its place was . . . envy.

Happiness in marriage is a moment by moment choice.
A decision to love, forgive, grow and grow old together.

Fawn Weaver, *Happy Wives Club*

in defense of totally ordinary love stories

lisa-jo baker

Give me an ordinary love. Give me morning hair and old, comfy pajama pants. Give me dirty socks next to the bed every night. Even if the bed is in different continents at different times and seasons of life. Even if the bed sags in the middle. Even if the bed is full of long, growing limbs and tiny, precious bad dreams that need to be comforted with blind kisses.

Give me an ordinary love. Even on its most boring days. Give me a dishwasher unloaded without fail every morning, noon, or night. Give me basketball practices he never misses and boys he always listens to. Give me LEGO patience and Polly Pocket fascination.

Give me an ordinary love. Give me sticky kisses over South African pancakes and dreams we worry over side by side.

Give me spreadsheets that project our future and tiny humans who clamber up and into our laps and laugh us away from our columns and into their bright blue skies of tomorrow.

Give me an ordinary love. Give me tiny feet on top of big, black dress shoes as he spins and she twirls and he watches her, with all that trust that spills out of her blue eyes and that he never drops. Give me pizza on Friday nights and hamburgers the way he makes them.

Keep your magazines and movie endings and mad dashes through airports—just give me an ordinary love. One that I can touch and hold and snort out loud with; that I can fight and fume and cry with; that I can trust and hope and dream with; that I can warm my feet up against under the covers at midnight.

Give me an ordinary love.

Keep your perfect endings and Pinterest prettiness and give me unshaved on Saturday mornings surrounded by the clutter of the week before and a good sense of humor as Elsa yells her morning greeting. Keep your RomCom expectations and give me the man who wipes snow off my windshield with a dishtowel because I can't find the scraper.

Keep your chocolates, flowers, and one-day-a-year on the calendar countdowns and give me every day, in and out and in again, someone who folds the laundry and sleeps in the bottom bunk bed because his sons believe that dads can punch bears. (I'll take your tulips, though.)

Give me an ordinary love I can kiss and hold and grow old with. Unselfconsciously. One that believes in commitment. That isn't afraid of change. Or wrinkles. Or this shaped-by-children waist.

Give me an ordinary love that sees my reflection in the eyes of my children and loves me just the way I am.

Give me an ordinary love that changes batteries and light bulbs, that drives the old car and mixes up the basketball times, that believes in the God of his father and mother and passes down the old stories to his sons and his daughter.

Give me an ordinary love.

Give me an ordinary love.

Give me an ordinary love.

Because with him, I'm who I want to be.

To love another person is to see the face of God.

Victor Hugo, *Les Misérables*

87

something that helps

deidra riggs

Early on, when we were first trying to figure out how a person was actually supposed to stay married "till death do us part" and (if I'm being honest here) wondering if the wedding vow people were serious when they wrote that line, H and I used to ask people who'd been married for any significant amount of time, "What's the secret?"

Sometimes people would shrug their shoulders and look at their spouse, then sigh and gaze at some point past my forehead, and that was that. Other times the couple would settle back into their chairs, reach across and hold each other's hands, and go on and on about one thing or another, telling us it was the absolute most surefire way to stay married to one another. "Don't go to bed angry," was a common theme, but H and I had already broken that rule. Multiple times.

Last week, when I looked at the calendar and realized our twenty-sixth wedding anniversary was quickly approaching, it sort of blew my mind to realize how fast the years had passed and just how much I really love the man I'm married to. I'm not saying we have a perfect marriage. Far from it. I'm not saying we are perfect people. Just ask our children. Or our parents. Or our neighbors. I'm not saying we even *like* each other all the time. We are experts at finding, wearing out, and grating on one other's one good nerve. But our love for each other isn't going anywhere. I don't have words to describe it, and if you asked me I'd probably shrug my shoulders and gaze at some point past your forehead.

I asked H, "Why do you think we've made it this far? I mean, we love each other for real. How did we do it? How *do* we do it? What, do you think, is our secret?"

H didn't have an answer for me then, but a few days later he said to me, "Remember your question? Remember how we were trying to figure out why our marriage has been so good? Why we've lasted so long?"

Of course I remembered.

"Well," he said, "I was looking at our wedding pictures. I was looking at all those people who came to our wedding, and those people? Those were some praying people," he said.

In my head, I recounted the people who had been guests at our wedding, and I had to agree with H. Those people were, indeed, some praying people.

"I think the key to our marriage," H said, "is that those praying people were praying for us."

Of course, that is not to say that the reverse is true. It doesn't mean that if our marriage hadn't worked that there hadn't been anyone praying for us. I don't think having praying people at the wedding is a magic formula that guarantees a successful marriage. But I do think it helps. (Not that one should try to stack the deck with praying people at a wedding. "Well, if we invite her, we have to invite two more pray-ers.")

"Wow," I said out loud, "that just changes my entire perspective on being a guest at a wedding. I mean, I usually just go and cry because it's so romantic and hopeful and beautiful." Now I see that being a guest at a wedding is an amazing privilege. Not something to be taken lightly. It is an invitation to celebrate and to dance and to cry and to witness the beautiful exchange of vows. And it is an amazing opportunity to bow for a moment and invite God to bless them and to keep them and to be gracious unto them—even till death do them part.

Celebrating twenty-six years of marriage today. Grateful for love. Grateful for the prayers of people who love us. Grateful for the hope that always lies ahead.

More things are wrought by prayer than this world dreams of.

Alfred, Lord Tennyson, "Morte D'Arthur"

choose what type of couple you want to be

shaunti feldhahn

I was speaking at a thank-you dinner for a group of people who work with married couples at a particular church. About two hundred small group leaders, counselors, and other marriage mentors gathered for music, a fun game show put on by the pastor and his wife, and then my talk as I shared some of my research about marriage. Encouraging research that shows there is so much more hope for marriage than we have thought. (For example, the 50 percent divorce rate is a myth.) I was sharing data these leaders could use to encourage their people to go "all in" in their marriages instead of giving in to the temptation to hold back and protect themselves—which creates worse problems!

91

So there I am, after the talk, interacting with these marriage leaders, and one man quietly comes over and says, "I need to share a story."

"Okay . . . ?"

He pulled me aside. "Five years ago, our marriage was disintegrating. I felt like I couldn't do anything right. My wife felt like I didn't care about her. We were constantly at odds, with one foot mentally out the door. And suddenly, one day, I stopped. I told her, 'There are two types of couples in this world. Those that want to work everything out before they commit, and those that want to commit to working everything out. Which do you want to be?'"

I was practically speechless—which, if you know me, is quite a feat. I knew I was hearing something profound. I stammered, "That is an amazing insight."

He nodded. "Yes, but not from me. I felt like God just gave it to me. And that is when everything changed. Because with the first approach, a marriage will never make it. You feel like with one mess-up, you could be done. But we decided we would commit to working everything out somehow. No matter what. And that is why we are now here today, with a great marriage, leading a small group of other married couples."

I scrambled for a pen to write down an insight that, in three sentences, was perhaps more important than anything I had said during my forty-minute talk.

In my research, I have seen the dramatic truth behind what this man said. The happiest couples are so happy, in part, because they take the risk of getting their hearts broken. They fully commit and fully invest emotionally instead of holding back to protect themselves; even if they don't know how they will work everything out, they know they have to! But then, because they know they will be together for the rest of their lives, suddenly they have drastically increased security. Suddenly, because of that security, they can be truly real . . . be vulnerable . . . be true friends . . . all of which usually leads to true happiness.

Follow this man's example and you'll probably find the same thing. Choose to be the couple that is all in and fully committed no matter what. It may be hard at times but it is life changing.

I will leave his words with you, again, so you can share them with others . . . and ponder your own answer.

There are two types of couples in this world.

Those that want to work everything out before they commit, and those that want to commit to working everything out.

Which do you want to be?

Real love, the Bible says, instinctively desires permanence.

Tim Keller, *The Meaning of Marriage:*
Facing the Complexities of Commitment
with the Wisdom of God

what i learned wednesday afternoon at the grocery store

dawn camp

Today I went to the grocery store around noon. At first I didn't understand why there were so many older folks, particularly older couples, and then it hit me: seniors get a 5 percent discount on Wednesdays. Although it wasn't my intention, I engaged in a considerable amount of people watching.

Fascinating stuff, these lives lived together for maybe half a century or more. I've invested over a quarter century into my marriage, so I was curious to see how it might look another quarter century from now. Here's what I observed.

Seniors Don't Worry about PDA

I saw hand-holding, arm caressing, a look in the eye, a stroke to the cheek. Twos who've become ones to that extent prefer to occupy the same space (even if it's in the grocery store). I wouldn't hold my husband's hand in public when we were dating, but public displays of affection seem to be quite the norm for the senior crowd; I think they've earned the right.

Do mundane moments deepen in meaning when you know there are fewer ahead of you than behind?

They're Driving the Cool Cars

As I climbed into my fifteen-passenger van, I couldn't help but notice an older couple loading up in a VW Beetle convertible and another in a Mini Cooper. Is this the payoff? Raise our kids and stay the course, together, and someday we'll stroll grocery store aisles arm in arm in the middle of the afternoon, riding away in a vehicle built for two? Maybe there's a fun little sports car in my future after all . . . who knows?

I drove away not only with a smile on my face but also a trace of envy for these seniors' slower pace, togetherness, and, yes, even their automobiles. Food for thought.

Grow old along with me! The best is yet to be.

Robert Browning, "Rabbi ben Ezra"

not today

diane bailey

We knelt before the priest for the Ash Wednesday service. I watched as the priest marked Doc's forehead with a cross of soot. Some of the ash fell from the priest's thumb and dusted the high spots of Doc's smile.

"From dust you came," the priest said, "and to dust you shall return."

It took all of my strength to keep my emotions from spilling down my artificial smile as the dark cross was made on my forehead.

The week before, Doc's regular checkup found a mass of irregular lymph nodes in his chest, and I heard the words said in quiet conversation: stage 3, maybe stage 4. Life seems to stop all motion when we are told the end of life is in view. We wake up each morning as if we have all the time in the world. As if we are eternal.

On the day I wore white from head to toe and he wore what he called *the penguin suit*, we vowed to love and stay together in sickness and health . . . until death. I said the words beaming with joy at the man who would be with me for the rest of our lives.

Our lives! *Not a singular promise but one that includes us both.*

Nothing in life gives a more sobering view of mortality than the word *cancer*.

A biopsy was scheduled. As we waited for the results, I began to prepare the house for a chemo patient. I scoured the bedroom, cleaning windows, curtains, and blinds. I washed everything I could safely press into the washing machine. Desperately, I looked for ways to stay in control of as much as possible. Fried foods were no longer on the menu because I was convinced that cooking lean and making smoothies from raw fruit were where I would take back my husband's body. And each afternoon we went to the gym. He needed to be as strong as possible before an intravenous poison would weaken his body to save it.

We would fight this evil trying to part us.

We vowed to stay together until we were separated by death, but for some reason I never thought we would need to use that part of the vow. We were married and in love, and surely this would last forever.

"More time, God," was my constant prayer as I scoured the house for anything that could cause a secondary infection to an immune system compromised by cancer and chemo. "I want more time with him . . . please don't take him from me

. . . not yet, not yet, we have fun plans for retirement soon. Please God!"

Doc laughed, and teased me about all this healthy eating killing him before the cancer did. He always finds the humor in any stressful situation because it is his way of giving comfort. He knows if I begin to laugh then I will lighten up and stress a little less. In our laughter he reminded me that God was still in control; what will be, will be. Then his hands began to rub the stress from my shoulders, and he kissed my face with tender encouragement.

Faith feels as if it wanes when knees buckle in fear and life changes, permanently, against your will. I used to think my faith was strong as I prayed for teens who ran through boundaries as if life were an obstacle course to be conquered. I felt my faith strained and prayer life increase as we chased them down at every turn, trying to keep them out of trouble until their brains matured into the adults we knew they could be. Now those seem like the good days in contrast to what we are facing.

I much prefer the vows that said, *for better* and *in heath*, not *in sickness* or *until death*. It wasn't until we were facing this crisis that I realized the word *forever* was never a part of our vows. The end comes to us all one day, and I am vehemently opposed to it. I want eternity with Doc!

The biopsy results came just hours before the Ash Wednesday service—benign. The lymph nodes were not cancer and could be easily treated.

Still kneeling at the railing of church, Doc turns toward me with ashes dusted across the high places of his cheeks, and my eyes, shimmering with emotion, embrace his. Returning his smile, I think, *Not today, Death. Not today.*

One day our bodies will return to the earth. One day we will make good on that vow to be parted only by death, and whoever is left behind will lean on the Lord to get through. But not today . . . no, not today.

The Lord is my light and my salvation; whom shall I fear? the Lord is the strength of my life; of whom shall I be afraid? . . . Though an host should encamp against me, my heart shall not fear: though war should rise against me, in this will I be confident.

Psalm 27:1, 3

with this ring
{part 2}

dawn camp

When Bryan and I moved back to family and Arkansas, we still wore matching bands, including the one recovered in a New Hampshire storm before the snow plow could sweep it away by morning's light. All that effort was ultimately for nothing, but we couldn't have known it then. And besides, it's all part of our story.

Our first child was born in the same town as me and my mother before me, entering this world one steamy June when the local forecast exceeded the high temperatures in Death Valley. We moved from one duplex to another because our air conditioner unit kept going out: too hot for us, much less a baby. I hold fond memories of that last duplex, the one before we moved to Georgia. It had a garage, which made us feel like grown-ups; a dependable air conditioner, which we'd learned to appreciate; and a Jacuzzi bathtub, which we wouldn't have again for many years. We bought our last cassette tape (Paul

Simon's *Graceland*) and our first CD (Wang Chung) and a big set of Cerwin Vega speakers, which we later replaced with an even bigger pair of DCMs. Filled with the awe and pride engendered by our impressive sound amplification capabilities, we could never have imagined the pair of fist-size Bose speakers that reach every corner of our home today.

Here I learned of the vigilance required to parent an active toddler, not knowing I'd do it seven more times. My mother feared my college days were over, like hers were when I was born, but soon college would take us to Georgia, robbing grandparents on both sides of easy access to their first grandchild (or great-grandchild). At twenty I didn't understand how hard that must have been, but now I've had a taste of it with kids of my own who've left for college.

Most people would have hated the sound of the interstate, separated from our tiny neighborhood by nothing more than a wooden fence. Not me. The desire to leave had drawn me to New Hampshire and would lead us to Georgia. But on a cold winter's evening during the brief period our marriage lived in Arkansas, the ring we fought so hard to find and braved a snowstorm to save disappeared during a simple trip to the grocery store. We searched the aisles, beneath the rows of baby food and boxed cereal, but we never saw it again.

And so for years Bryan wore as his wedding ring a gold nugget ring he'd owned before we married. We were sad our bands no longer matched, but happy to have a free solution. Little did we know, the story of my husband's ring wasn't over and would conclude with a gold band more perfect than any we could have imagined.

To be continued . . .

for better, for worse

For better, for worse, for richer, for poorer, in sickness and in health . . .

Traditional Wedding Vows

the story of us

laura parker

We got married a dozen years ago when we had just barely turned legal to drink a glass of wine, and everyone said we were too young. But we would just roll our eyes at each other behind their backs.

We picked out invitations and cake flavors in the same month we studied to pass our college exams. And older marrieds told us to "get ready for that first year," because it was going to be the "hardest year of your lives." And we would smile and say thank you, and then roll our eyes behind their backs too.

Because we were young and madly in love, and we wouldn't believe a word anybody said about marriage being a *struggle*. All we saw was that we wouldn't have to say goodnight to each other anymore and that we'd soon have license to decorate our own kitchen.

And when we heard the statistics during our engagement about how half of all marriages end in divorce, it wasn't a reality that registered on our crazy-for-each-other radars. Because *how could people grow apart? And how could marriages become a battlefield? And how could affairs even happen?* We rolled our eyes at the unbelievability of something so wonderful as a marriage crumbling.

But youth and early-years love have a way of painting optimism in broader strokes than reality. And I'm glad for that, really. Because who wants to start a race believing you'll end up losing? Who wants to walk down the aisle assuming it's going to get awful?

But twelve years in, I have learned that *awful* it will, indeed, sometimes be.

There are kids and bills and baggage that you didn't know existed. There are losses and disappointments and turns you never signed up for, and there is always a dance of selfishness that plays out in a million different ways and with a trillion different hurts.

And you can't get pregnant. Or you do and then you miscarry.

You leap for the job and then it falls apart.

You have the kids and never realized that they would take such center stage.

And the pressures of grown-up living can push you into separate corners, and separate sides of the bed, before you even realize what's happening.

Twelve years in, and I have learned that marriage can be hard and intimacy takes work. It demands the front burner and it is always, always costly. A marriage is not a relationship built for autopilot, not one to pay attention to *after* the kids are gone, not something handed to you—but rather something fought hard for.

And I watch young people I adore begin to get married. I see the same optimism in them that I had a dozen years ago. But I don't roll my eyes at them—not at all.

Because I know they're about to start writing their history together. And a history, *together*, is a much more powerful thing than a white dress or a kitchen of their own, anyway. It takes longer to get, sure, but it's an ocean deeper too.

And that, *that*, is something worth a heavy dose of optimism.

Love is life. All, everything that I understand, I understand only because I love.

Leo Tolstoy, *War and Peace*

how i saved my marriage

richard paul evans

(Dedicated to my sweetheart.)

My oldest daughter, Jenna, recently said to me, "My greatest fear as a child was that you and Mom would get divorced. Then, when I was twelve, I decided that you fought so much that maybe it would be better if you did." Then she added with a smile, "I'm glad you guys figured things out."

For years my wife, Keri, and I struggled. Looking back, I'm not exactly sure what initially drew us together, but our personalities didn't quite match up. And the longer we were married the more extreme the differences seemed. Encountering "fame and fortune" didn't make our marriage any easier. In fact, it exacerbated our problems. The tension between us got so bad that going out on book tour became a relief, though it seems we always paid for it on reentry. Our fighting became so constant that it was difficult to even imagine a peaceful relationship. We became perpetually defensive, building emotional fortresses around our hearts. We were on the edge of divorce and more than once we discussed it.

I was on a book tour when things came to a head. We had just had another big fight on the phone and Keri had hung up on me. I was alone and lonely, frustrated and angry. I had reached my limit. That's when I turned to God. Or turned *on* God. I don't know if you could call it prayer—maybe shouting at God isn't prayer, maybe it is—but whatever I was engaged in I'll never forget it. I was standing in the shower of the Buckhead, Atlanta, Ritz-Carlton yelling at God that marriage was wrong and I couldn't do it anymore. As much as I hated the idea of divorce, the pain of being together was just too much. I was also confused. I couldn't figure out why marriage with Keri was so hard. Deep down I knew that Keri was a good person. And I was a good person. So why couldn't we get along? Why had I married someone so different from me? Why wouldn't *she* change?

Finally, hoarse and broken, I sat down right in the shower and began to cry. In the depths of my despair, powerful inspiration came to me: *You can't change her, Rick. You can only change yourself.* At that moment I began to pray, "If I can't change *her*, God, then change *me*." I prayed late into the night. I prayed the next day on the flight home. I prayed as I walked in the door to a cold wife who barely even acknowledged me. That night, as we lay in our bed, inches from each other yet miles apart, the inspiration came. I knew what I had to do.

The next morning I rolled over in bed next to Keri and asked, "How can I make your day better?"

109

Keri looked at me angrily. "What?"

"How can I make your day better?"

"You can't," she said. "Why are you asking that?"

"Because I mean it," I said. "I just want to know what I can do to make your day better."

She looked at me cynically. "You want to do something? Go clean the kitchen."

She likely expected me to get mad. Instead I just nodded. "Okay." Then I got up and cleaned the kitchen.

The next day I asked the same thing. "What can I do to make your day better?"

Her eyes narrowed. "Clean the garage."

I took a deep breath. I already had a busy day and I knew she had made the request out of spite. I was tempted to blow up at her. Instead I said, "Okay." I got up and cleaned the garage for the next two hours. Keri wasn't sure what to think.

The next morning came. "What can I do to make your day better?"

"Nothing!" she said. "You can't do anything. Please stop saying that."

"I'm sorry," I said. "But I can't. I made a commitment to myself. What can I do to make your day better?"

"Why are you doing this?"

"Because I care about you," I said. "And our marriage."

The next morning I asked again. And the next. And the next. Then, during the second week, a miracle occurred. As I asked the question, Keri's eyes welled up with tears. Then she broke down crying. When she could speak, she said, "Please stop asking me that. You're not the problem. I am. I'm hard to live with. I don't know why you stay with me."

I gently lifted her chin until she was looking in my eyes. "It's because I love you," I said. "What can I do to make your day better?"

"I should be asking you that."

"You should," I said. "But not now. Right now, I need to be the change. You need to know how much you mean to me."

She put her head against my chest. "I'm sorry I've been so mean."

"I love you," I said.

"I love you," she replied.

"What can I do to make your day better?"

She looked at me sweetly. "Can we maybe just spend some time together?"

I smiled. "I'd like that."

I continued asking every day for more than a month. And things did change. The fighting stopped. Then Keri began asking, "What do you need from me? How can I be a better wife?"

The walls between us fell. We began having meaningful discussions on what we wanted from life and how we could make each other happier. No, we didn't solve all our problems. I can't even say that we never fought again. But the nature of our fights changed. Not only were they becoming more and more rare but they lacked the energy they'd once had. We'd deprived them of oxygen. We just didn't have it in us to hurt each other anymore.

Keri and I have now been married for more than thirty years. I not only love my wife, I like her. I like being with her. I crave her. I need her. Many of our differences have become strengths, and the others don't really matter. We've learned how to take care of each other and, more importantly, we've gained the desire to do so.

Marriage is *hard*. But so is parenthood and keeping fit and writing books and everything else important and worthwhile in my life. To have a partner in life is a remarkable gift. I've also learned that the institution of marriage can help heal us of our most unlovable parts. *And we all have unlovable parts*.

Through time I've learned that our experience was an illustration of a much larger lesson about marriage. The question *everyone* in a committed relationship should ask their significant other is, "What can I do to make your life better?" *That* is love. Romance novels (and I've written a few) are all about desire and *happily ever after*, but happily ever after doesn't come from desire—at least not the kind portrayed in most pulp romances. Real love is not to desire a person but to truly desire their happiness—sometimes even at the expense of our own happiness. Real love is not to make another person a carbon copy of one's self. It is to expand our own capabilities of tolerance and caring, to actively seek another's well-being. All else is simply a charade of self-interest.

I'm not saying that what happened to Keri and me will work for everyone. I'm not even claiming that all marriages *should* be saved. But for me, I am incredibly grateful for the inspiration that came to me that day so long ago. I'm grateful that my family is still intact and that I still have my wife, my best friend, in bed next to me when I wake in the morning. And I'm grateful that even now, decades later, every now and then one of us will still roll over and say, "What can I do to make your day better?" Being on either side of that question is something worth waking up for.

Forgiveness is not a feeling; it is a commitment.

Gary Chapman, *The Five Love Languages: How to Express Heartfelt Commitment to Your Mate*

notes on a marriage

shannan martin

Cory and I hightailed it up to Michigan on Sunday to belatedly celebrate our fifteenth anniversary.

We used to get away together more often . . . back when life was different in lots of ways. Upon reflection, we've only had one night alone in the past eighteen months where we weren't as sick as a couple of hound dogs. Summary: we were long overdue.

For two nights we stayed up late, slept in late (our dream schedule!), ate fantastic food cooked by *not me*, read books, strolled around, held hands, took selfies, ate snacks, took naps, adventured, and generally had a blast together. We also hot-tubbed.

The first night we talked about the kinds of things that require mental energy reserves and zero interruptions; important things like mission and little kids and big kids, community, church, and our friends sitting in the county jail. We'd caught a breather, so we regrouped and dreamed without restrictions, our faces barely lit, feeling bold and gutsy in boiling hot water under sheets of stars like the ones in the movies.

Just before my face started to throb (my signature symptom for "you've had enough hot tub, Martin"), I flashed back to thirteen years ago, sitting at my end of our blue-striped couch, bawling my eyes out because I was in a mess of a marriage and I couldn't see an end.

I wanted out. Everything felt hopeless. All I could imagine was an eternity of unhappiness. Things had spiraled so quickly and I was terrified of the shifting ground. I felt unloved, unlovable, and very alone. (And everything I felt, Cory probably felt double.) Right there, against the backdrop of my misery and the dingy paint job of our "economical" apartment, God shoved past my junk and told me the truth about things. *See how hard the enemy is fighting to destroy you two? Just imagine what he's scared of. Just imagine the good you'll do with Me, together.*

In that instant, a page turned. I felt the slip of paper under my fingertips, heard the rustling brush of words on words, saw, for the first time in a good, long while, some white space. Room for a future. I had no idea it was what I wanted, what I'd been looking for.

That was the beginning of this, right here. We couldn't possibly have imagined it. We moved to DC, resoldered our mangled commitment to each other, got jobs in politics, hitched our stars to the American Dream, went to church, paid our tithe, adopted babies, and bought a farm.

I clung to those cheap-carpet words whenever I felt tremors beneath our fine-tuned life. I decided our little ones were the "good" we were doing together. And they were. Still are.

But I had no idea there was more. I didn't imagine a future of loss and instability and surrender and loneliness. I didn't dream of a little house on a shabby street, a failing public school, or that my husband would spend his days with criminals but call them his friends.

In my wildest wishes, I couldn't trace the shape of a tall kid with an ankle bracelet and a heart broken for so long he thought it was *supposed* to feel that way. Back then, I thought bigger was better and more was more. I thought Jesus kept His best gifts on the tallest shelf, so I climbed. With my husband.

It would have been foolishness to imagine that our greatest purpose, our near-tangible peace, would look like bits of broken dreams. But in that hot tub, as I was wearing a ridiculous bikini, skimming the bubbles with my fingertips, and staring at my man, it clicked into place. It crystallized.

This life, right here, this was part of God's purpose for us, inked before the first bloom of time.

It's not so exceptional. It's not the kind of life they make movies about. To us it is ordinary. It is grueling, some days. It can feel thankless and annoying, and sometimes boring to its core.

All those gifts I mentioned, the ones I didn't even know to ask for, they aren't because we did anything right or because we're very smart in the ways of righteousness. They are grace. Only grace. The kind that makes you fall to your knees. The kind that makes you remember your depravity. The kind that makes you believe God can meet you in your darkest hour, sit down beside you on your secondhand couch, and tell you to shape up and cut the drama, already. There's work to be done, but you've got to drop that torn-up net you're holding and follow Him.

Cory and I have talked about that moment plenty of times, but it felt good to say it all again, in order. Bubbles blurred the edges of all our words, and there we were: one set of brown eyes, one set of blue. Still locked on each other when common sense would have said otherwise.

God defies gravity, friends. He laughs at our foolish "logic" and our made-up psychobabble. He holds our world at what seems like a scary-sharp angle and tells us it's level.

What feels real to us often isn't, and only when we take a hard look at His unbending love for us and His endless mercy for us, only when we're so desperate that we actually listen, can we begin to see straight.

That's the kind of weekend I had.

I believe that the world was created and approved by love, that it subsists, coheres, and endures by love, and that, insofar as it is redeemable, it can be redeemed only by love. I believe that divine love, incarnate and indwelling in the world, summons the world always toward wholeness, which ultimately is reconciliation and atonement with God.

Wendell Berry, *The Art of the Commonplace: The Agrarian Essays*

grace, mercy, and cheesesteaks

crystal stine

$\mathcal{I}$t all began September 22, 2000. My husband, Matt, and I are that ever-rarer breed of high school sweethearts. We began dating the September of our senior year of high school and have been best friends ever since. That's more than fifteen years together. I'd like to tell you that it was love at first sight, that we knew immediately we would be together forever and married with kids and the white picket fence.

But I don't live in a Hallmark movie. So it looked a bit different for us. The truth? He used to date my twin sister, and I used to date his best friend. Yep. All kinds of awkward in that sentence. And let's not forget that Matt was incredibly mean to me when I was dating his best friend—I actually didn't like him at all during tenth grade. But with patience and God's grace, by the time our junior year was ending we were good friends.

When we finally thought we might want to date one another, it was almost time for our senior year to start. I was college-minded and wasn't particularly interested in having a boyfriend when I started my freshman year at Villanova. Matt didn't really see a problem with it. I wanted to travel, go away for college, and be independent; Matt was (and is) more comfortable staying around home, near family. I wanted to get a degree in something fabulous, like international relations, and work in a big city; Matt was going to a Bible college with plans to be a teacher in our hometown. I didn't have a lot of faith in marriage—my parents had divorced and remarried; Matt's parents have always been together.

But one night, over AIM (oh, yes—we grew up on instant messenger), Matt made it too obvious to ignore and wrote, "I like you. You like me." It was the internet version of "please check *yes*." I couldn't disagree with him. And that was how it all began.

Isn't it interesting to see God's hand in this situation, fifteen years later? God worked to transform this heart of mine from apprehension to acceptance, from independence to something that began to look like Christlike submission. My marriage is a blessed testament to God's grace and mercy.

Because that long-distance relationship we chose to pursue? It was hard. We were, at minimum, an hour apart for five years. There were distractions, opportunities, fights, surprise visits, new friendships, broken relationships, separate experiences, growing up, and growing closer to God. Looking back, I would do it all again because now I can see how God was preparing us to learn what commitment looked like in marriage. What it would mean to have and to hold, to be there for one another when it was hard even more than when it was easy. While we were in the midst of it? Only God's grace and our determination to find a way to make it work kept us together.

The Saturday night before Easter in 2005, Matt proposed. Here's a confession: I didn't make it easy on him. Bless his heart. I'd come home for the weekend and it was *freezing* outside. I was in sweats, all ready to be cozy and stay inside, and this man of mine decided that we just had to go outside and sit on the front porch swing. Seriously? I'm ashamed to admit that it took a lot of convincing—and I was *not* happy about it. So out we went, and he started nervously saying all these sweet things, and I still wasn't getting it—I was just annoyed and cold!

Finally he got around to ask me to marry him, even after all my whining and complaining, and I said yes. We set our minds and hearts toward a final and permanent goal while we were in college, and it has translated well into our mind-set for marriage. We have one option now: make it work (thank you, Tim Gunn). And there have certainly been challenges to that goal over the last ten years.

Compromise

We chose to move back to our hometown after college to be closer to our families, even though I wanted to stay near Philadelphia. We rented a house beside my grandparents and across from my parents, even though we wanted to buy our own place. We took jobs we had to have to make money, not because they were our dream jobs.

And now? I love living near our families. We have the best friends and mentors anyone could ask for. We own our first home, our "gotta take it" jobs have led to our dream jobs, and we get to visit Philly a few times a year. I can't go long without a cheesesteak!

Fear

I was afraid of a lot leading up to our wedding. I didn't have the best outlook on marriage. I was afraid of losing my independence and having to learn to be submissive, and, most of all, afraid of failing at being the type of wife Matt deserved.

God has done a great work in this girl's heart and shown me what it's really like to be the type of wife the Bible instructs us to be, and it's a joy, not a burden. My independent streak is still there—it's how God created me—but He's been gently showing me how to use it to build His kingdom and not my own.

Trust

We would not have survived a five-year long-distance relationship without trusting one another 100 percent. Being honest, doing what we said we would, and being faithful during the dating portion of our relationship have helped us to be trusting in our marriage. Because we knew we could trust one another, we have created space in our relationship where we can share the hard things and believe one another when we extend grace and forgiveness.

As difficult as our college years were, they have only sweet-
ened our first ten years of marriage. We're far from perfect. But
together we've chosen to travel on the road full of progress—
which is so much sweeter than the impossible road of perfec-
tion. For better or for worse.

Compromise, if not the spice of life, is its solidity. It is
what makes nations great and marriages happy.

Phyllis McGinley, "Suburbia: Of Thee I Sing"

a peek into my everyday marriage

emily t. wierenga

The other night we left the boys with my sister and rented a hotel room in the mountains. We planned to snowboard the next day.

We bought some beer and takeout and I couldn't rest that night. For hours, we lay there in our separate beds, because the room came with two, but I couldn't sleep. And I cried.

Trent stretched out his hand across the space between our beds, his fingers reaching for me in the dark. "Hold on to me, Em," he said. "I'm here."

We're not exactly John and Yoko.

Trent's a math geek and I'm a literary nerd. He's loud and I'm quiet. He's athletic and I run into walls. We both like books. We both love camping. And we're both over-the-moon crazy about each other and our boys.

But marriage has come hard for us. Hard, with years of anorexia and insomnia and fists punching the wall.

I'm putting away the laundry, the seven loads Trent folded for me while playing a computer game, because between my books and my boys, I can't seem to take a shower or do any house cleaning, let alone fold the laundry.

And I'm putting the baskets away when he calls "Suppertime," because Trent's made burgers, and on the table is a salad with peppers and grated jalapeño cheese, lettuce, bacon bits, and grated carrot, and chopped onions that always make Trent cry—it's the only time I see him cry—and "I made you fancy salad," he says.

Like my friend says, there's nothing sexier than a salad-making man.

But truth is, *I'd be a wreck without my salad-making man.*

The one who held me those long, skinny anorexia years.

Our best conversations happen over a board game because games are Trent's love language, and we're still getting the intimacy thing.

I used to fight him when I got mad, sometimes with my fists, and he'd shake his head and grab my wrists and then finally leave. Slam the door and drive off while I wept into the couch pillows, but that doesn't happen anymore.

No man is perfect, and Trent will say things that unintentionally hurt me, or he'll forget to take out the trash, but I will also do things—like forget his birthday, as I did one year—and ours is the kind of marriage that throbs with love.

The kind of love that will not give up: not through anorexia, not through insomnia, not through moves to Korea or moves home to take care of parents with cancer, not through slammed doors or tears or fists, because there's also the salad. There's the laundry. There's Trent taking the kids to his parents so I can write. There's him reaching out in the dark to hold me, to pray for me.

I want the kind of marriage that dances into its golden anniversary, that kisses each other on wrinkled cheeks and laughs at each other's jokes long after the sun has wound down.

And maybe the secret is to never stop reaching out in the dark. To never stop taking hold of each other's hands. And to never let go.

Not even for a moment.

Love is not affectionate feeling, but a steady wish for the loved person's ultimate good as far as it can be obtained.

C. S. Lewis, *God in the Dock*

we make beautiful amends

alia joy hagenbach

I read a post on the internet in which a writer talked about her divorce, the packed boxes, and the pain and brokenness that come from separating a life. I sucked in air at her beautiful agony. I think I held my breath until the end. I hoped for a happy ending, a "but God," a "to be continued." But sometimes we get none of these things.

Maybe life will go on in brokenness and God will work in the fragments because He is so good. Maybe we are being redeemed day by day, and I still hope that the boxes will be unpacked and sorted and he and she will settle and find their home together. I don't even know them. I met her once, this blogger with kind eyes. I've read her story the way we often do on the internet and felt participatory in the outcome. Or at the very least in the journey. I whispered a prayer for them and I felt like crying.

I can't help think it's a mistake to think a divorce means new beginnings and rebirth, however painful, instead of the death of a sacred thing. But mostly I felt like crying because I could have written that post ten years ago.

We've had a rough week of marriage. We clash and bruise and pull back. Where my temper used to blaze like wildfire, I simmer now, stew on the silences, pull to the furthest corner of our bed and turn my back like a fortress. Sometimes words seem like too much effort after all these years.

Sometimes it comes in patches and I remember how different we really are. I remember how we were kids; I was a fresh-faced teen hovering on the brink of a womanhood that would overtake me with children and duties and loneliness. He was broad-shouldered with sun-kissed hair and the bluest eyes.

I believed he would be enough. But he never was, not from the very beginning. Maybe he believed this too. Maybe he had no idea what he was getting into. In fact I'm sure of it.

I find the years have taken their toll and those broad shoulders have carried burdens when I was bedridden and sickly, when depression clutched my soul and I whispered prayers into my damp pillow as tears slid down my cheeks and pooled in my matted hair. And for a while he would whisper how beautiful I was and stroke my back like I was a temperamental child, but eventually he gave up.

And it broke him a bit. How unfixable I was. This wearing down of life and the daily siren of a 6:00 a.m. alarm to jolt him awake to black skies, the frozen winters where his palms would split like broken ground, and paint would etch itself into the cracks from the construction of a life held together by shutoff notices and paychecks never stretching far enough and so much backbreaking work. He labored methodically, faithfully, and he smiled less and drank more.

He married a girl who aged in despair to some foreign thing, bent and warped and sharp-tongued.

And the boy who became a man under the pressure—I didn't know him at all. We grew up side by side but not together.

And even though I don't know that writer's full story (how can anyone ever know the full story), I could have penned every word about aching loss and mistakes and the misery of a marriage gone sour and stagnant on my tongue. And so I mourned the loss of her marriage. I ached with it because I know that place.

But God.

There is only that. I can't say anything formulaic as to why, even when there are hard weeks, there is also the space his body fills as he pulls me to him. And I fit there. The whole of me in his arms being made complete year after year, fingers draped across those shoulders. I can't explain in twelve steps how to go from the brink of divorce to the fullness of sixteen years and the anticipation of a lifetime more.

Only God in the seams reinforcing glory could ever explain the way a man and woman make love last a lifetime. We are a partnership built of sorrow and grace and joy. I know now what I never knew as a girl: these things are not opposed. We find our filling in God alone and only then in each other. We are never enough.

My mind has been tempted with all the ways I chose poorly, or he did, when we said "I do" and committed our lives without having any idea what that meant. But we know now.

We know we said our vows once, but we say "I choose you" every day. I will never stop choosing him. We are students of forgiveness, ever learning to say sorry and always making grace in love. We make beautiful amends. We choose—and I won't lie and say it's easy, because so many days it's not.

But sometimes we make it look easy. Sometimes I ease my shoulders back into him and he wraps his arms around me and whispers in my hair and I giggle, just like that girl. Sometimes he watches me, his eyes trailing me across the room as I hoist children and laundry baskets and my ordinary life, and his grin gets wide and boyish again and I know those looks. He still believes I'm beautiful. He still sees something in me I need reminding of.

Sometimes I welcome him home and I've memorized every crease in his brow and I know when he needs me to rub the ache from his shoulders. I trace the corners of his frame and I feel the tension ease up and I know then we've built a whole life together.

We don't fit; we were never right for each other. Not for one second. How can two broken people in a sin-stained world do anything but make each other bleed? Only grace, only God. I don't know any other way, and this way is hard and demanding yet so full of beauty and joy I cannot contain it.

It is a gift and a trial and I accept it as both. I set my face toward God and pray in the silences when the days are hard and we are blistering edges, rubbing and chaffing, and I pray for the worn places, the paths walked through the years together. The making of our love. This week we celebrate sixteen years of marriage, and I thank God for all of them, even the ones we almost quit.

I can say, with confidence, "To be continued . . ."

For his anger endureth but a moment; in his favour is life: weeping may endure for a night, but joy cometh in the morning.

Psalm 30:5

tending hope

kelley j. leigh

Even when things look futile and dead on the outside, usually, somewhere buried deep inside, there is hope for new life.

Black Bear and a Broken Tree

I bought a half-dead tree several years ago during an end-of-season-clearance sale at the hardware store. I knew better. But it seemed a reasonable risk for the price.

I dumped the short, twiggy weeping crab apple tree out of its sad little plastic bucket and transplanted it near the downspout, in a hidden, sheltered corner of our house, safe from high-altitude winds and dry extremities. I gave it fussy attention, hoping for a piece of my Midwest roots to bloom in this pine forest of the Rocky Mountains.

Four years later, early morning coffee pot burbling quietly in the kitchen, I leaned over the sink to peer out the window and admire the first batch of tiny red apples on the now-thriving tree. My loud gasp startled the dog at her bowl. She froze, water dribbling off her chin, and looked at me with a cocked-head question. *What? What's the matter?* Heavy paws ran behind my sock feet as we both dashed out the back door.

Fresh bear tracks in the soft garden pathway led to the tree. During the night, my ten-foot tree had been snapped in half by a hungry black bear. The top limbs were sheared clean of apples and left in a wilted pile on the gravel. I imagined the portly bear sitting on his bottom, legs outstretched with heavy padded feet, gorging extra calories for the winter ahead, cleaning off branches the way a panda strips bamboo. The lower half of the broken tree looked like a stunned middle-school girl in the first minutes after a very bad haircut.

Sometimes the Things We Plant Don't Bloom as Planned

Over the years, my husband and I have had our own hard shearing and pruning conversations about things other than trees. We have well-practiced angry dances about things like sex, intimacy, and weedy threats to our marriage. Depending on the issue, usually one of us threatens with the huge loppers while the other stands by with wringing hands.

Now and then we all need a healthy pruning. Certain old growth needs to be cut back, tossed out so fresh, better life can grow—which is why I decided to keep the bad-hair-day tree and help it recover.

A few weeks back, a small herd of deer, including some sweetly spotted twin fawns, took to wandering our forest neighborhood. When nobody was watching, the deer munched up any available leafy garden growth. Most of the new leaves on my barely recovered crab apple disappeared. With just one lone twig still standing, the tree was forlorn and naked like a plucked chicken perched on a barnyard fence.

How Long to the Point of No Return?

My husband and I have been in similar naked plucked-chicken stages of our marriage, barely surviving, pruned down to the last vestiges of all that we believed. We have lain in bed next to each other, together but lonely, insecure and apart, hearts left for dead. Over the course of many autumns, we have walked together through intimate crises into healing. In the process, I've come to believe that only God can prune and tend the unseen places of our hearts in unexpected ways; ways that bring beauty beyond recognition. It's a seasonal process that looks like my over-pruned crab and includes feelings of point-of-no-return ugliness and death.

But, in my limited experience, I can say this with confidence: if Jesus is at the center of the tending, new life branches out, and Spirit-breathed fruit grows. It does.

Certain autumn nights, when my bedroom window is open and the breeze is just right, I look up at the stars and wonder if the bears are hibernating yet. I slide my heat-seeking body under my husband's heavy, sleeping arm and remember when I used to be afraid of him, of being intimate, of the much-needed pruning in our marriage. I feel his breath on my face and feel thankful for the pain that came before and all the stolen fruit and broken days that preceded this blooming season.

And that's why the apple tree will stay. Even if I know that bears will come and limbs will break. As Martin Luther is purported to have said, "Even if I knew that tomorrow the world would go to pieces, I would still plant my apple tree."

great expectations

For I know the thoughts that I think toward you, saith the LORD, thoughts of peace, and not of evil, to give you an expected end.

Jeremiah 29:11

thanks a lot, jane austen

ashleigh slater

When you release expectations, you are free to enjoy things for what they are instead of what you think they should be.

Mandy Hale

I was completely captivated by the beauty of his words. They were tender, heartfelt, poetic. "You must know—surely you must know that it was all for you. . . . You have bewitched me, body and soul."

Too bad these words were written by a woman.

I'd gone to see the movie version of *Pride and Prejudice* with my three sisters. It was a bit strange to sit there, the only married woman of the bunch, and watch as the Bennet sisters sought their potential mates. After all, I no longer wonder how, where, or when I'll meet my husband. To borrow a popular phrase: *Been there. Done that.* And frankly, I'm glad.

Glad that instead of waiting eagerly for "Mr. Right," I now can marvel at the wisdom of God's matchmaking, putting together two people who complement and challenge each other.

But being the married one of the bunch also has its drawbacks. I'd lost the ability to believe men could be romantic in the way Jane Austen penned them. Once the film ended, it took a few minutes for me to pry myself from my seat. I wanted to bask in the glow of Mr. Darcy and Elizabeth's romance. The romance filled with words I didn't hear on a daily basis. Words that were much more romantic than, "Are the dishes in the dishwasher clean?" or "Did you get a chance to wash my white T-shirts?"

As we left the theater, I turned to one of my sisters and said, "Real men don't talk like Mr. Darcy." And that's all it took for discontent to set in. I began to examine how the romance between my husband and me had seemingly disappeared.

During our courtship and engagement, my husband, Ted, had expressed his affection with homemade cards, roses, and words that made my heart flutter. In fact, he verged on the poetic. But once we got married, after two babies in two years, he was too busy putting together swings, heating up bottles, and installing car seats in our newly purchased minivan even to think about romantic gestures. And the cards, roses, and poetic words dried up.

Now my mind began to concoct other reasons for my husband's lack of romance. Could it be I'd become boring? Unattractive? Did he see me only as the mother of his children and not the love of his life? Perhaps my sweatpants and ponytail weren't as alluring as I'd thought.

I spent a few days brooding in unhappiness and doubt. Until the clouds parted and I had a revelation. Mr. Darcy won Elizabeth's heart not with flowery words but with actions. He salvaged her family's name and gave the encouragement that led to her sister's engagement, and it was the very living out of his love that brought Elizabeth to admit her true feelings for him. This is exactly how my husband goes about winning my heart day in and day out: with his actions. Maybe he isn't so different from Mr. Darcy after all.

Too many people miss the silver lining because they're expecting gold.

Maurice Setters (attributed)

the date night dress

dawn camp

It happened on a Friday night as we drove into town for dinner and a movie. While scrolling through Instagram I saw an online friend's stunning selfie: sexy summer dress, perfect hair and makeup, fun jewelry and strappy sandals. She'd dressed for a date night with her husband, and I knew he must feel like a lucky man. As I looked down at my mom capris and flip-flops—what I was wearing on our date night— my husband didn't seem quite so lucky.

I left a comment on my friend's Instagram post: "You've outdone me. On my way out and don't look like this," and then showed my husband the picture.

"Maybe I need a trip to TJ Maxx," I joked, but I wasn't really kidding. My husband took an earlier exit than the one we needed and I thought he'd taken me seriously, but we were only stopping to gas up the car.

"Why don't I shop while you get gas?" I proposed, hopeful. Money was tight at this point in our marriage—so I was asking for an indulgence—but my good man, clearly intrigued, dropped me at the door and drove away. I quickly grabbed a few dresses and headed for the dressing room. A striking black and white number fit like a charm, but then I looked down at my flip flops and knew I could never wear them with it.

"I found a dress, but I would need new shoes too," I called and explained to my husband.

"Just do it, and go ahead and get new lingerie too."

I found a chunky pair of tall black wedges unlike anything I owned. They were so out of character that I posted a picture to Instagram and Facebook captioned "Yes or no? #pleaseadvise." My date night dress adventure began with an online prompt, so why not continue with one? I received an assortment of replies, ranging from "No, please, no!!" to "Yes! So fun!" Ultimately, the yeses won and I walked out with a new dress, heels, lingerie, and even an impulse bag of gummies at the check-out (although obviously the whole purchase was an impulse).

We pulled into a dark shopping center parking lot where I slouched down in my seat and changed clothes. (I can't tell you how much my husband loved all of this.) When we walked into the restaurant, I noticed the self-satisfied, she's-with-me look on my husband's face. Whenever I stole a glance at him at the theater, he was already looking at me. All evening I felt admired and appreciated—and maybe a little overdressed— but as special as I felt, I knew my husband felt it equally. We're always told that men are visual. Dressing to please him seemed to show my love for him on a whole new level.

Date nights are our love language, and most of the time I still walk out the door in a pair of jeans, but on those rare occasions when I take an extra minute to dress to impress my husband—maybe in the same little black-and-white dress and chunky heels—his response is always worth the effort.

The happiness of married life depends upon making small sacrifices with readiness and cheerfulness.

John Selden (attributed)

the most romantic
gesture ever

mary carver

In my high school Valentine's Day was quite the floral spectacle. Like all adolescent boys everywhere, my classmates knew that buying flowers on that infamous greeting-card holiday was mandatory if they hoped for any chance of having a girlfriend on February 15.

Rather than interrupt class with deliveries all afternoon, some wise person in charge of our school decided that the best course of action was to simply place all flowers and gifts on tables in the cafeteria. Then, following the last bell, students were responsible for checking the tables.

That meant that if you had even an inkling that someone might have sent you flowers, you had to walk slowly by the tables, eyes darting back and forth, searching for your name on a box or bouquet. *It was an outrageous form of teenage torture, and I can't even believe it was legal.*

As a long-time victim of Just a Friend Syndrome who had recently acquired a Boyfriend Who Is Not Romantic At All, I was fairly certain my name was not on any of the smelly flowers. *And yet, I hoped.*

I don't remember exactly how I found out there were flowers for me on the table. Did I see them as I walked by, oh so casually, after class? Or did someone else see them and tell me? I don't know. But I do remember exactly how I felt when I saw the roses.

The world stopped. My heart soared. Angels sang. *You get the picture, right?*

Mark gave me a dozen red roses that year—and also gave my mom a rose too. *Are you kidding me?* Could anything possibly be more romantic than that? At seventeen years old, I thought not. Clearly, this was The Most Romantic Gesture Ever.

A little over a year later, I went to stay at the lake with about half of my class a few days before graduation. We water-skied, swam, shopped in the tourist-trap town, and even got one of those old-timey pictures taken. And after dinner each night, we gathered in the resort's dance hall for an awkward, are-we-in-middle-school-again dance.

As we hung out, waiting for the second night's party to start, one guy punched me in the arm and asked me to save him a slow dance. Since this particular guy was one I'd had a crush on since middle school, I said, "Sure." And I said it real cool-like, you know. Even though I might have possibly been shrieking in my head, *I WILL SAVE YOU ANY DANCE YOU WANT!*

(And yes, for those of you keeping track, I did still have that one-time rose-buying boyfriend who would become my husband. He was at home. I was at the lake. I have no excuse or explanation for those treacherous and embarrassing shrieking thoughts.)

So the dance started. And it was kind of lame. My friends wanted to go back to our cabin and hang out, but I couldn't leave. *I had promised that guy a dance!* So I waited. And waited. I waited as he danced with pretty much every girl in the room—except me. Finally I snapped out of my idiocy and realized this whole thing was stupid. As one more slow song started and that guy grabbed Another Girl Who Was Not Me, I turned (in a huff, I am sure) and walked out.

I ran to catch up with my friends, who had wisely decided not to wait for me. And then I heard, "Hey! Wait!" I felt a hand on my shoulder and I turned around. That guy had followed me outside. And he said, "Let's dance."

Had more romantic words ever been spoken?

Look, I know. But in the moment? It was Billy Crystal running across New York City at midnight. It was Tom Hanks taking Meg Ryan's hand on top of the Empire State Building. It was John Cusack holding up that ridiculous boombox. *It was romantic.*

(Yes, even though it went nowhere and meant nothing. I promise. For those of you keeping track.)

For years I held on to memories like this and stories like that. The roses and the stupid dance and all the things we're programmed to "need"—that was my definition of romance.

And every time my husband (he of the dozen-plus-one roses, remember) failed to live up to that definition, I felt so disappointed, so ripped off.

Where were my flowers? My surprise getaways and weekly date nights and notes "just because I love you"? The dances under the stars, the carriage rides in the park, the champagne and mix tapes and feeding each other chocolate on a Thursday?

Yeah, I wasn't getting any of that.

And it took me a long time—*too long*—to figure out that those things are not all they're cracked up to be. Those things mean nothing compared to someone who kisses you and never mentions your morning breath, who puts up with your mom and says of course your best friend can go on vacation with you and adores your daughter like nobody's business, who holds your hair and goes to the store for feminine products and brings you a glass of water when you throw a grown-up tantrum and cry yourself dehydrated.

But even though I (eventually) figured that out, I didn't immediately become immune to Romance Envy. It still flared up every now and then, often when reading gag-inducing Facebook statuses or watching unrealistic chick flicks. (Am I alone on this?)

However, I think I was cured for good this spring. It seems like this year has been the "big" anniversary of so many couples we know. Ten, fifteen, twenty-five years our friends have been together, and they've celebrated right. Vacations, cruises, flowers, wine, and all that jazz. Oh, yeah, probably jazz music too.

Mark and I celebrated our anniversary in May. Well, not so much "celebrated" as "made it to." The weeks leading up to the big day were filled with arguments, threats, silence, and tears. So, on the thirteenth anniversary of our wedding, we went to our first counseling session together.

It was by far the most romantic thing Mark could have done.

He made the appointment. He vowed, all over again, to stay with me forever and do whatever it takes to make our marriage work. The issues that brought us to that point aren't important to this story, and we both share the blame for it all. What matters is that we chose to stay, to fight, to find love again.

Most. Romantic. Gesture. Ever.

Love never fails.

1 Corinthians 13:8 NKJV

the good wife

how i (thought i) failed my marriage

ann swindell

$\mathcal{I}$ had been crying regularly for three weeks when Michael gave me the ultimatum.

"Either you quit something or I'm going to quit it for you." His voice was filled with compassion, but it also carried an edge. "You're going crazy, Ann, and you're taking me with you."

I burst into fresh tears. "I can't quit anything, Michael! I have to work and I'm not quitting school and you know I'm not going to stop being involved at church! And—and—there are always dishes!" I paused for a second before continuing, "We're only three months into marriage and I'm already failing!"

In the time since Michael and I had gotten married, I had started graduate school as a full-time student, was working two jobs, had responsibilities at church, and felt the new and added burden of trying to keep our apartment sparkling and make dinner every night, not to mention trying to learn what it meant to be a wife. I was trying to do it all and was, in my mind, failing—the apartment was a mess, I was too exhausted to cook on most evenings, I was fighting to stay up on my graduate work, and I was constantly stressed.

"Ann, you're not failing!" His voice softened. "*We* are not failing." Michael was concerned. "Where are all of these expectations that you're putting on yourself coming from? It's not like I care if everything is perfect in the apartment or if dinner is on the table every night. Who are you comparing yourself to?"

And the lightbulb went on: my mom.

A Realization

My mother is one of my best friends. She is bright, beautiful, and has more energy than anyone I know. She is also a spectacular wife, employee, hostess, small group leader, cook, and church member. On top of that, she only needs about five hours of sleep every night to be able to get up and do it all over again.

In that moment, God revealed the expectations that I had unwittingly and unconsciously placed on myself. Somewhere, deep down, I went into marriage believing that in order to be a "good wife," I needed to be my mother. I never spoke the thought, never even realized how much I believed it, but it was coloring our young marriage.

My mother is a fantastic cook, and when I was a child, she had homemade dinners on the table nearly every night, so I assumed I should be able to do the same thing. Mom always got the dishes done after dinner, so I thought I ought to be doing that as well. She worked part-time and was completely capable of opening our home to school and church groups in the evenings, and so I expected the same thing of myself. It wasn't that my mother or my father or even Michael required these things of me—they all, in fact, told me to not put so much pressure on myself. But my mother was the model I grew up with, and I had internally swallowed her wonderful capabilities and took them on as expectations for myself that neither God nor my husband asked of me.

Michael squeezed my hand. "Ann, I didn't marry your mom. I married you."

That night began a process of allowing God to come into my heart and change the expectations I had placed on myself.

My Own Identity as a Wife

A conversation with my mother on the phone continued that process. I was talking with her about making dinner for my husband and my sister, who lived near us. Being from a family who loves food, we started talking about the details of the meal.

"So what are you making tonight?" Mom asked.

"Chicken potpie, I think." I hesitated. "And I found a pumpkin bread boxed mix at the grocery store that I'm going to try." As far as I knew, my mother had only ever made pumpkin bread from scratch.

My mother's response shouldn't have surprised me, but it did. "Great idea, honey! When you find something that works and saves you time, go for it."

"Yeah." I paused. "Yeah, it is great."

Apparently, she could tell I was uncertain. There was a smile behind her voice. "Anything you can do to simplify your life is wonderful, Ann. Take advantage of things like that as often as you can."

"Thanks, Mom. It's good to hear you say that."

And it was. So along with pumpkin bread mixes, this is what I am embracing in myself. I am a woman who requires at least seven hours of sleep a night, a woman who doesn't need to have a perfectly clean home, a woman who is happy to pop a frozen pizza in the oven, a woman who needs time every week to *be* rather than *do*.

I decided to quit one of my jobs, and—by God's grace— started learning that the definition of being a "good wife" is one that I am going to be carving out for a long time. Now, seven years later, Michael and I are still growing in our roles as spouses, learning the give-and-take of being married. God has enabled me to see that who I am (and who I will be) as a wife may be very different from who my mother is as a wife. Not better or worse, just different.

Knowing My Identity in Christ

This is a lesson that I've needed to continue to learn. The world I live in is constantly telling me I'm not good enough in one way or another, or I need to be someone different than who I am in order to be a "good wife." Because while I will never be my mother, I will also never be a lot of other things. I will never be a gourmet cook for Michael or our family. I will never have an immaculately clean house. I will never wear a size 4 dress. I will never look like a fashion model. I will never have it all together all the time. But I will feed our family fresh and healthy food. I will provide a safe and loving home for my husband and daughter. I will wear lovely and appropriate clothing. I will stay active and strong. And I will be okay with being a work in progress.

As a wife, I will never be my mother and I will never be my sister. I will never be my friend Gwen, and I will never be anybody but myself. Being a good wife, for me, means being a good wife *to Michael*, the one particular man out of billions whom I married. And I believe that God has equipped me to be the best wife for him, just as I believe God has equipped him to be the best husband for me. I don't need to be some-one else—anyone else—to be a good wife. In fact, I need to be exactly who I am to fulfill all of the purposes God has for my life, and being a wife is part of that.

There is another side, however, to this process of becoming secure in who I am as a person and as a wife. Because the flip side of being content with my own gifts and quirks is that I *do* need to change—but not into a different size dress or into a gourmet chef or even into my mother. I need to change more and more into the image of Christ. I cannot write off my sin and my selfishness simply as "being myself." I can't avoid transformation because my brokenness is "who I am." On the contrary, anything in my life that does not reflect the love, compassion, and grace of Christ *does* need to change. But the only one who I am being made in the image of is Jesus Himself. No other expectation—from myself or from the culture I live in—should shape me.

And as I continue to learn what it means for me to be the type of wife God created me to be, I am finding that I have more respect for my mother today than I have ever had before. I understand that she did a great amount of challenging and meaningful work for our family. Now that Michael and I have a child, I admire her even more for the love and sacrifices she poured into us. Within that respect for her, I am discovering freedom in my own heart and life. Loving and admiring my mom does not mean that what is best for my marriage is for me to be exactly like her. So, as Michael and I seek to walk in God's love in our marriage, I've found that while I'll be using my mother's recipes until the day I die (pumpkin bread

recipe excluded), the best thing for us is for me to be free to say that I'm not my mother—I'm myself, with quirks and capabilities of my own. And that, Michael reminded me, is exactly why he married me in the first place.

Patience gives your spouse permission to be human. It understands that everyone fails. When a mistake is made, it chooses to give them more time than they deserve to correct it. It gives you the ability to hold on during the rough times in your relationship rather than bailing out under the pressure.

Stephen Kendrick, *The Love Dare*

a kind wife

joy forney

About a year ago I sent my husband a list of things that I thought that he might like to see me do around the house. I asked him to put the list according to priority, from greatest to least.

Here is the exact list I sent to him:

clean, ironed laundry

yummy meals including lunches

fresh, homemade bread for your sandwiches

keeping up with emails

thank-you notes

outreach in the community

hospitality/having people over

making sure there are cookies or something yummy for
you when you get home (including tea)

a clean, picked up house

And this was his exact response:

Thanks, but I would rather have you put aside anything/
everything you have to do in order to start each day with the
assumption that I LOVE YOU, and therefore anything I do
or say is given the benefit of the doubt that I LOVE YOU.

Get enough rest and say no to enough activities so that
you have the energy to be NICE TO ME (and the kids) when
I'm home.

Honestly, I appreciate the rest of it, but don't really care
that much if it comes at the expense of the first two things
up at the top of the list. Maybe you think that I think you're
a bad wife or mom if you don't do this stuff. If so, that is
wrong. I would much rather have a messy house, make my
own lunches from white, store-bought bread, have no snacks,
etc. etc., but have a nice, happy wife who likes me, than the
other way around.

So, to sum it all up, showing me you love me has more to
do with WHO you are than what you do! It's my best friend
I fell in love with and want to hang out with, not my maid!

You see, I was so busy doing things for my husband, trying
to be the perfect wife, that I was getting it all wrong. I was so
tired and stressed that I was snappy, unkind, and impatient.
And the only thing my dear husband wanted was a girlfriend!

Am I saying that it's wrong to do things for your husband
or family? Of course not! But I am saying to think about
keeping "being kind" as your *top* priority.

I have learned my lesson. I have stepped back in many areas in my life in order to have margin and rest, so that I am not overstressed and my husband (mostly) has a kind, gentle, loving wife.

I know what it is to live entirely for and with what I love best on earth. I hold myself supremely blest—blest beyond what language can express; because I am my husband's life as fully as he is mine.

Charlotte Brontë, *Jane Eyre*

sometimes happily ever after doesn't start out the way you planned

dawn camp

Most girls spend years dreaming of their wedding days—or so the story goes. I dreamed about where I'd go to school and what I'd study. My big book of college profiles was worn and dog-eared, a compass intended to point me in the right direction after high school graduation.

Just when I thought I'd figured it out—in May of my senior year with an acceptance letter from an Ivy League college in hand—I met the seventeen-year-old brother of a friend from a rival high school and everything changed.

I fell so hard and so fast that by August it was difficult to load up the U-Haul with my family and drive eighteen hundred miles from home. From him. As much as I loved the school and the new friends I made, nothing could overcome the constant ache in my heart. We became engaged the following March and married in October, in that New Hampshire town where he'd gone with me back to school and rented a basement apartment nearby.

Although I never doubted the man I chose, for years I'd sit in the pew at weddings and wonder if I missed something by getting married in a school chapel, in a dress I bought off the rack in that college town, with the justice of the peace presiding and a school newspaper photographer.

Sometimes I'd begrudge the bride who'd return from her honeymoon to move into a new house. Our first four children were born before we owned an actual home of our own.

I'd forgotten that God specializes in conceiving great things from humble beginnings: a shepherd boy who would be king of Israel; a Jewish orphan who would become the queen of Persia and save her people; His own Son, born in a manger inside a stable.

Whether your wedding was big and fancy, small and simple, or hasn't yet occurred, let me share these truths:

Your wedding isn't about the dress or the reception. It's about the man. The vows.

Your marriage isn't about where you live or what you drive. It's about loving your husband (which is commanded of us, as an act of the will). Two becoming one flesh. Commitment.

Don't be ashamed of simple beginnings (or simple middles and endings, for that matter). Sometimes happily ever after doesn't start out the way you planned or could ever imagine.

Be content with such things as ye have: for he hath said, I will never leave thee, nor forsake thee.

Hebrews 13:5

invitation to dance

lynn d. morrissey

When my husband, Michael, finally retired after thirty-seven years of faithful service to the same agency, I was elated. I've always felt that companionship is the foundation of a good marriage, and envisioned adventures for Michael and me to pursue *in tandem*—writing and speaking on marriage, gym workouts and bike rides, travel, and cooking and dance classes. *Vive* variety!

But, wisely, Michael took a hiatus before plunging headlong into my plans for his new life to catch up on house repairs, declutter, and try to organize his beloved wife of forty years: *moi*. (This pursuit may consume his lifetime.)

Reluctantly I acquiesced, realizing that everyone needs a time-out to regroup during major life transitions—especially one as significant as moving into one's legacy years.

But I also knew that after reflection comes risk. I didn't want to push Mike into doing what he didn't desire to do, yet I also saw gifts in him that he didn't recognize. If I knew anything about legacy living it was that *now* was the time to make a difference for God's kingdom. And as married partners, we could have greater impact serving God together. I knew we needed to relish every magnificent moment, living colorfully and daringly, because life is short.

So I dusted off a poem called "Invitation to Dance" that I had written for Michael a few years earlier to remind him that *now* is always the time to dream and to dare.

The autumn before I had presented it to him, Michael and I were picking apples at a local orchard, and for reasons I can't explain, a sudden urge swept over me. I don't know if it was the invigorating air or the apples' pungent scent or the rows of trees queued up like participants in a line dance, but I had to enter in. I had to dance—*just dance*, oblivious to how I looked, unintimidated by who was looking, uninhibited by what I feared. I longed to grab my partner's hand and weave a waltz through a trellis of trees.

But Michael wouldn't dance. He wouldn't enter into the moment, because he thought he couldn't. And despite my coaxing, and my "It doesn't matter whether or not you think you can dance or who might be watching" plea, he was immovable.

Mike *would not budge.*

And it's at that moment that I knew this was more than an invitation to dance. I was daring him to enter a reckless adventure with me, his wife, to kick up his heels in delight, to abandon rules without thinking, to move without knowing the steps, to risk looking foolish when people gawked, to live far away from the guidelines and sidelines of life.

A good marriage is not a solo endeavor. We are united in a lifelong commitment, and I can think of no better way to honor it than to dance through life together, enjoying it as an adventure of beauty and delight. And there is no better time to dance than *now*.

Note: the painting to which I allude in my poem is called "Carnation, Lily, Lily, Rose," by British mid-nineteenth-century artist John Singer Sargent. Not satisfied to paint by memory, he gathered all his supplies, hauled them outdoors, and painted at dusk—that ethereal, twilight hour when sunset melts across the sky, fading quickly to black. Desiring to paint in an Impressionistic manner, using only natural lighting, he worked feverishly, taking advantage of those fleeting, magical moments. It took two years to complete the painting, and he gave his all during those few moments each day. I saw a metaphor in how he worked.

Invitation to Dance

"I don't dance in apple orchards," you say,
with a straight face, then a smile,
but all the while, my hand extends to yours.
"Come," I say, "please dance."
But you won't bend.
"I don't dance in apple orchards," you stress.
And then, you wink.
But dare I ask again?
I know that you are resolute,
and I know that life will end
in an absolute blink, in the time it takes
for these apples, weighty with August's wine,

165

to loosen from limp stems in a gust of ruthless wind
and fall and bruise and roll and roil into bubbling
    decay.
"I don't dance," you say.

But if not *now,* then when?

And if not here, between these choreographed rows
    of
red-lanterned trees, festooned for plein-air dance
(like Sargent's lanterned garden all aglow with
    twilight),
then where?

The painter highlights the evanescent hour,
and daily, feverishly dances transient light onto
    canvas,
knowing magic soon will end.

Is it possible to compress beauty?

Yes.

He does.

We *must.*
I dare to ask again:
Will you thrust yourself into my arms and commence
    this *pas de deux?*
Don't fret about the steps.
Let the magic lead . . .

All life's a dance
begging you to enter in,
to move in its embrace.

Take your cue:

Trace how the apples dance from breeze-swayed
    boughs
before they fall.

They whisper,
    "Now.
    Please, now.
        Please now."

————————

The night seemed to fade into blossoming dawn
The sun shone anew but the dance lingered on
Could we but relive that sweet moment sublime
We'd find that our love is unaltered by time.

Al Dubin and Dave Franklin,
"The Anniversary Waltz"

the refining power of marriage

Love is a commitment that will be tested in the most vulnerable areas of spirituality, a commitment that will force you to make some very difficult choices. It is a commitment that demands that you deal with your lust, your greed, your pride, your power, your desire to control, your temper, your patience, and every area of temptation that the Bible clearly talks about. It demands the quality of commitment that Jesus demonstrates in His relationship to us.

Ravi Zacharias, *I, Isaac, Take Thee, Rebekah: Moving from Romance to Lasting Love*

when you'd like to stay in love

holley gerth

$\mathcal{I}$ think of my marriage, now ten years old. When we did premarital counseling, all the charts said we were opposite— "*incompatible*." But we didn't care. We were young and in love. So we said "I do" and we learned what those differences between us meant in everyday life. How being very emotional (me) and very practical (him) can cause us to rub up against each other like sandpaper.

But funny thing about sandpaper—*over the years it makes the rough places smooth when it's in God's hands*. Those differences? That incompatibility? I wouldn't trade a thing for them now. They've become some of the greatest strengths of our marriage.

We took another relationship assessment recently. This time? "*Highly compatible. Vitalized marriage.*"

We laughed out loud about that one for a long time. We grinned at what God can do. My husband is a good man—strong, steady, kind, and a faithful friend to me. Maybe I've got some positive qualities too. But what I'm learning is that the best way to find love, and to stay in it, is to keep running back to the God who *is* love.

Only He can transform our weaknesses into strengths. Only He can take two broken, fallen people and teach them how to love each other well. (*And let me tell you, I can be a stinker to live with sometimes.*) Only He can take a couple through over six years of storms and make their marriage come out stronger on the other side.

Love is more complicated and more worth it than I could ever have imagined ten years ago.

Perfectly compatible? Happily ever after?

Sounds pretty boring to me.

There is no more lovely, friendly or charming relationship, communion or company, than a good marriage.

Martin Luther, *Table Talk*

the marriage marathon

kristen welch

He slows down his pace so I can catch him. I'm breathing hard. Hurting. My legs feel like dead weight. Every step is sheer determination.

He gets ahead of me and circles back so that we are in step again. Together. Terrell's watching me out of the corner of his eye. He motions for me to keep going. He hands me water. He wills me to take another step. I am tethered to him and I can feel my husband mentally pulling me toward the finish.

I used to say I hated running while I sat on the couch with a sweet tea in my hand. Now I say it while I'm running. I was not made for this. It doesn't come easy. It's hard.

"Just a little farther. You can do it," he says loudly over his music.

"You're not my coach," I snap at him.

Oh, hey, so I'm also sort of angry when my legs are on fire. I make a mental note to thank him for cheering me on later (you know, when I can talk again).

We are a team. We run together. When I lag behind, he encourages me. When his body suffers, I support him. Some runs are easier than others, but most are long and hard with no end in sight.

Running reminds me of marriage. Marriage is not a quick sprint, it's a slow, long, and sometimes painful marathon. We have been running this race together for twenty-one years. We've had very good years and very bad ones. This last one stretched us and pulled us apart in ways we didn't expect. It's revealed new areas of weakness that come with transition and overwhelming work. The need to find each other again has driven us closer, desperate to finish this race well.

There are moments on the road and in marriage when I think it would be easier to just quit. As I struggle my way through the cold wind; painful shin splints; and arguments over money, kids, and work; I find myself asking, *Why am I doing this?* And then I remember the commitment I've made. The one to God, to me, to him.

And I keep going. One step after another. We keep running this race.

A few months ago, Terrell was given an ultimatum by his doctor concerning his diabetes. Since then he's lost another twenty pounds and he signed up for a half marathon to raise money for Mercy House. My husband is running for his life. And I'm running because I'm on his team. And that's what teammates do—they support each other.

Recently, Terrell wrote me a letter that outlined my life accomplishments. And yes, an empty laundry basket might have made the list. Because that actually happened one time. Some days I don't give him a lot to work with.

As I read his words, I couldn't stop the tears. Because every single thing on his list that looked like my achievement was actually *ours*. Every word I've written, every story I've told, every meal I've made, every positive parenting moment, every woman I've remembered in poverty, every last thing—he was in my corner, slow clapping, whispering in my ear in my most inadequate moments, "You can do this, Kristen. Don't stop. You can do this."

I am running for him. I am running for us. I am running because I love running when it's over. Nothing makes me feel more like an overcomer than finishing what I've started. With every step, I can hear my heart pound. *I can do this. I can do this hard day. I can do the hard work I've been called to.*

Marriage is hard, redeeming work. I've discovered my ugliest, weakest moments with this guy by my side. I have whined and wallowed and wept in his arms. I have waged war against this man. He knows me at my worst and still chooses to run this race with me.

And that's worth finishing for.

My husband has made me laugh. Wiped my tears. Hugged me tight. Watched me succeed. Seen me fail. Kept me strong. My husband is a promise that I will have a friend forever.

Fawn Weaver, *Happy Wives Club*

is love supposed to be fair?

angela nazworth

"All's fair in love and war" . . . or so goes the old saying that traces back to John Lyly's *Euphues*, written in 1578. For centuries, the adage has granted individuals license to cheat on battlefields both literal and of the heart.

Ironically, any soldier who has fought for his or her country will tell you that there is nothing fair about war. No matter the reasons for entering a fight, terror and ugliness abound savagely. But I'll leave the subject of war for other writers to discuss. Love now weighs heavily on my mind.

Contrary to Lyly's famous line, the only commonality I know that exists between love and war is that neither is fair. Yet, unlike in war, the unfairness of love can add unfathomable beauty.

Love in its purest, sacrificial form has never been fair. I don't think it was designed to be fair. As God sculpted Adam from the fresh earth, He knew that His most glorious creation would break His heart. Yet still, God breathed man to life. It was not fair, but the beauty surrounding such love could not be denied.

When the world knew only darkness and despair, God sent hope in the form of His son, Jesus Christ. The sinless man and true embodiment of love was scorned, spat upon, rejected, beaten, and killed by a method that glorified cruelty as sport. The image of my sweet Savior nailed to a brutal cross swells a lump in my throat. It was the greatest atrocity committed by humankind, one in which I bear some of the blame.

It was not fair.

But the beauty . . . the stunning, breath-stealing beauty pouring from such sacrifice cannot be denied.

Fourteen years ago this week, my life changed when my boyfriend of only four months sent me on an elaborate treasure hunt that ended with him on bended knee. The night I agreed to be his wife, as well as during the wedding-planning months that followed, delusions of fairness occupied an enormous space of my mental real estate. And as we exchanged vows, slivers of cake, and many kisses I envisioned all the bliss the next fifty years could possibly hold. Oh, I knew that our life together wouldn't be perfect, but I was confident that it would at least be fair.

Less than two weeks after my wedding day, I learned that my previous notions were laughable. Fifty-fifty? Equal give-and-take? Those are just good-intentioned but flawed concepts. Our marriage experienced illnesses that rattled our faith, emotional pain that rammed us to our knees, and losses that ransacked our haven. Not only did life hit us with some

177

unjust blows but we also dealt each other some unscrupulous punches. That's what human beings sometimes do when life gets gritty. We mess up. We make mistakes. We get angry with each other. We cause unwarranted pain.

My marriage is not and has never been fair, but it is worth fighting for and it does hold beauty that cannot be denied.

Arms open to embrace one in need of forgiveness . . . beautiful.

Fingers entwined as a new life swallows her first gulps of air . . . beautiful.

Tears cried for the one who aches . . . beautiful.

Hands steadying the one whose body is ravaged by pain . . . beautiful.

Laughter echoing throughout corridors . . . beautiful.

Feet that stumble as they walk a rugged path but also glide as they dance . . . beautiful.

Lips that touch softly as evidence to both passion and commitment . . . beautiful.

Love. Unbridled, agape love, a love that is taught by its Creator, is not fair. But its glorious beauty cannot be denied.

⸻

If I speak in the tongues of men or of angels, but do not have love, I am only a resounding gong or a clanging cymbal. If I have the gift of prophecy and can fathom all mysteries and all knowledge, and if I have a faith that can move mountains, but do not have love, I am nothing. If I give all I possess to the poor and give over my body to hardship that I may boast, but do not have love, I gain nothing.

1 Corinthians 13:1–3 NIV

five keys to having a strong marriage—even during the storms of life

crystal paine

Since we've moved to Tennessee and restructured the way we do life, I will be honest and tell you that it's been a challenge for our marriage. It's brought a lot of new issues to the surface and we've had many long, hard talks (and yes, some out-and-out arguments) as a result.

As we've struggled through together, our marriage has grown and it's been good. Not *easy*, mind you, but good. And I know our marriage is going to come out stronger as a result.

Working through these things and not giving up until we find resolution and oneness has made me appreciate our marriage even more. Some days we might be at odds and frustrated with each other, but because we are both committed to our marriage "till death do us part," these storms are making us stronger instead of ripping us apart.

If you're going through a tough time in your lives right now, I want to share five keys that have helped us to have a strong marriage—even during the recent storms of life.

1. **Stop Coasting.** A good marriage doesn't just happen; it requires a *lot* of work and time and effort. Just like you couldn't expect to build a muscular body without putting in a lot of time weight lifting, so you can't expect to have a strong marriage if you're not constantly building it up. Make time for your spouse. Go through your day looking for ways to build up your spouse, encourage your spouse, and love your spouse. If you're too busy to invest in your marriage, you're just plain too busy.

2. **Don't Keep It G-Rated.** Seriously, people. You are supposed to be lovers, not roommates. Act like it. Look for ways to keep the spark alive. Flirt with your spouse. Whisper sweet nothings. Think about what you used to do when you were dating, engaged, and newlyweds and bring some of that romance back into your marriage. Truly, what happens in the bedroom will affect just about every other area of your life. In most cases, if you make romance a priority, it will clear up a host of other problems and issues.

3. **Find the Good and Praise It.** There are always a host of things we can point out, pick at, nag, and criticize. If we spend all our time focused on the negative, we'll be frustrated by how far short our spouse is falling from

where we want them to be. On the flip side, there are always, always, *always* good things to praise. Become a noticer of the good. Go through your day looking for things to be thankful for about your spouse. These could be little, everyday things or big, major things. The more you focus on the good, the more good you'll probably see.

4. **Ask Forgiveness Often.** A good marriage is built around a lot of humility and the ability to say, "I was wrong, will you forgive me?" Those are hard words to say but they are necessary. We all make mistakes. We all say words we shouldn't say. We all respond in anger at times. When that happens, be willing to admit you are wrong. Don't stuff things and just try to be extra nice to make up for your shortcomings. In addition, don't blame your spouse. Owning our own mistakes and apologizing for them is the first step in restoration.

5. **Learn Their Love Language.** While I don't like to box people into specific categories, every person has a unique love language—the way they feel most loved. If you're unfamiliar with the five love languages, they are Words of Affirmation, Acts of Service, Receiving Gifts, Quality Time, and Physical Touch. In many cases, you'll be a mix of a few of these, but you'll almost always have one that is dominant. Once you know what someone else's love language is, it really helps you to be able to demonstrate love in a manner that means the most to them. For instance, my dominant love language is Words of Affirmation. It means the world when Jesse tells me

how much he appreciates me and how proud he is of me. This speaks love to me much more than buying something does. Jesse's love language is Quality Time. It's very important to him that we spend time together and just be together—without me acting rushed or like I'm busy. As a Type A person who does not have the love language of Quality Time, it's been a learning experience for me to figure out that just *being* with him is extremely meaningful to him.

It's taken us years to figure these things out about each other, but as we've put forth effort to learn each other's love language and to be intentional about expressing it, our marriage has grown much stronger. And it's been every bit worth the effort!

Only with time do we really learn who the other person is and come to love the person for him- or herself and not just for the feelings and experiences they give us.

Tim Keller, *The Meaning of Marriage: Facing the Complexities of Commitment with the Wisdom of God*

i just got engaged and immediately doubted my decision

here's why i still said "yes"

mo isom

Our whole lives we're sold "happily ever after," time and time again. In the movies. On TV. On Facebook, Pinterest, YouTube. I've heard talk about "Prince Charming," "The One," and "Soul Mates." Even in church, I've been told that God was designing the perfect man for me. That there was *one* out there who would complete me.

And while I've always rolled my eyes at these concepts, I failed to realize how much they were etching their way into my thoughts and heart.

I've been in a relationship with Jeremiah for fifteen months, and I've known I wanted to spend my life with him for six. We've navigated the highs and lows of dating. We've stumbled and struggled . . . a lot. We've had great victories and highs. We've cried some, laughed often, bickered more, and smiled the most. We've supported one another in the struggles of building our careers. We've each seen financial blessings at times and we've each been broke-as-a-joke at times. We've been faithfully committed to one another and held one another accountable to purity. We've wrestled conviction and repented openly to one another. We've praised and worshiped together, we've struggled and sinned together, and we've crawled back to the foot of the cross together. We've fallen in love with one another's families and we've wasted days away dreaming of our own future family. We've worked out together, vegged out together, and rocked out together. We've worked through book studies with one another, traveled with one another, and been beyond annoyed with one another. We've comforted one another, danced with one another, and respected one another. We've navigated through this past year and ultimately, every day, chosen to grow in love with each other.

And yet when Jeremiah took a knee and asked me to be his wife, I immediately doubted my answer.

I know I'm not the only girl in the world who has cried tears of joy with a new ring on her finger while wrestling the overwhelming weight of the "yes" that just escaped her lips. I know I'm not the only girl whose mind began spinning when the hypothetical dreams became the reality of the moment. I know I'm not the only girl who wondered why her "fairy-tale" moment wasn't as ridiculously blissful and simple as the four hundred thousand movies made it seem. And I know I'm not the only girl who has ever felt guilty for even harboring this range of emotions.

But the fact of the matter is that as soon as the boyfriend I cherished became the fiancé I promise to cherish for the *rest of my life*, my human nature began to doubt. And I began to realize how much my mind and heart had been crafted by the world rather than the Word.

You see, the world says there is a soul mate. The world says there is a Prince Charming. The world says there is a *perfect* person for you out there, and if you find him you will live happily ever after. If you marry the wrong one it's not the end of the world—you can just divorce him and continue the hunt for the man made *just* for you. The man who will always make you happy. But if you want the least amount of hassle possible, make sure you find the perfect one the first time around.

The world says the person should be perfect for you. The ring should be perfect for you. The proposal should be perfect for you. The wedding should be perfect for you. And the Pinterest world will certainly praise you. (If you manage to host the perfect barn wedding, that is.)

But the Word says it has nothing to do with you. The Word says the covenant of marriage has everything to do with God. The Word says the journey of navigating a lifetime promise has everything to do with Jesus. And the only thing perfect for you in the equation is *grace*.

You see, my mind doubted because I was weighed down with the fear of making the wrong choice. Maybe Jeremiah wasn't "The One." How would I know for sure? There are things we disagree on. There are things about him that don't always make me happy. It's been a challenge, at times, loving him. And I know it's been a challenge for him to love me. Maybe we're just compatible and I'm making the wrong decision. How do I know, for sure, that he is my soul mate?!

But maybe we've got it all backward. Marriage is a covenant—a promise—to God that you vow to love another like Christ first loved us. In the most intimate, challenging, all-inclusive way. A vow to become one flesh with another person. To serve them and selflessly love them as Christ served and selflessly loved us all the way to the cross. To carry their burdens. To take the lashes of their shortcomings. To bear the taunting of their sins and struggles. To put them before yourself to the point of brokenness, so that we can ultimately rise, just as our King did, in love. With a greater understanding of the magnitude of the gospel. With a greater appreciation for the power of what Jesus did on our behalf.

Marriage is a taste. A tiny, intimate taste of God's love for us. It is a promise that is not taken lightly because, ultimately, it is a promise to accept another and love another like God loves us, daily. It is nothing we can even come close to doing on our own. And *that* is the joy of saying "yes" to the proposal. Not that we have found the "perfect person" but that we are a step closer to drawing back a layer and getting to see God's perfect love played out in a beautiful way in our lives.

I am excited about marrying Jeremiah because he is *not* the perfect man for me. And I am not the perfect woman for him. But we are both committed to following the perfect King who showed us the perfect example of how to love.

It is overwhelming, to me, that God would allow me—messy, baggage-carrying, selfish, emotional me—to have the honor and privilege of loving and caring for His sweet child Jeremiah. I know that the minute I believe I'm capable of selflessly and unconditionally loving him, I will fail. But it brings the sweetest joy to my heart to know that I don't have to go at it alone. That God is with me. God is with us. And through Him, all things are possible.

But Jesus beheld them, and said unto them, With men this is impossible; but with God all things are possible.

Matthew 19:26

made for each other

embracing your differences

sheila wray gregoire

In my marriage, I tend to be the one who wrecks the cars. Keith wrecks the laundry, but that doesn't cost nearly as much. For a while there I seemed to have a string of issues needing little bumper touch-ups, and the mechanic helpfully suggested that he could install those little floaty-things that boats use to the outside of our car. Keith thought this was hilarious. I did not.

Of course, Keith recently backed into a tree and shattered our van's rear windshield, but since this was his one and only automobile infraction in our whole marriage, we viewed it as an aberration rather than a pattern. So when he went to buy a new car this fall, he bought a standard—also known as a manual or stick shift, for the Americans out there. I can't drive a standard. So I can't drive his car. I'm still trying to figure out if there's some hidden meaning there.

Keith and I have other differences too. Keith has the "all the lights in the house must be turned off if not needed" gene. I'm missing that one. His idea of a relaxing afternoon is to actually relax. I like taking energetic bike rides. He likes war movies. I like Jane Austen. We're a strange pair.

And yet, after twenty-three years, what most often occurs to me is how alike we've become. Who we are, I believe, is partly a function of who we grow to be as we walk, day by day, with those we love.

People who know me may be surprised by this, but I tend to be on the shy side. I didn't speak outside of the house until I was seven. Today I make my living speaking at women's events and retreats, often in front of large groups, which doesn't bother me in the least. But parties, where I have to talk to people one-on-one, are stressful. How do I keep the conversation going? I don't find it natural at all.

It's not natural for Keith, on the other hand, to shut up. And as we've been married, he's taken me to so many parties that I've begun to open up. But he's also started to quiet down. Had we not married, he might have been even more gregarious and I may have become even more introspective.

Or take food. I crave sweets, but not fat or salt. Keith, on the other hand, once drank a cup of bacon grease because someone dared him. I often have a craving for vegetables. Keith had to force himself to start eating them regularly. If Keith hadn't married me, he'd likely be a lot heavier than he is right now. And I'd probably still never know how wonderful real butter makes everything taste.

I've always loved to travel, and even before we were married I had seen a lot of the world, saving up my money from my jobs as a teen to tour around overseas. But my trips were confined to museums and tourist attractions. Keith, on the other hand, likes to get to know people. Over our years together we've ventured farther abroad, most recently to Kenya. Within five minutes he knew our driver's life story. The porter in our final hotel told him all about his education. Keith finds a way to draw out people I would never have normally talked to, and I'm gradually learning also. If I had followed my initial instincts, we would have seen the world but only from a distance. And if Keith had followed his, we never would have seen it at all.

Over the last twenty-three years we have changed. I am not the same woman who walked down that aisle, and he isn't the same man who was waiting for me. I loved him dearly then, but I love him much more deeply now. I think we make a mistake when we search for that soul mate, the one person who completes us. The more I think about it, the more I think that we become each other's soul mate. Just by being with each other, we change each other.

It isn't a matter of finding the perfect person as much as it is becoming the perfect couple. Compromise. Spend time together. Stretch yourself. You just may find that you're becoming made for each other, after all.

So often we think that when our marriages don't work it means that we married the wrong person. But I don't think there is a right person. I think you become the right person the more you commit to each other and stick it out. You aren't born "made for each other." You become "made for each other" as you adjust to each other with grace.

Change happens gradually, but it will happen more dramatically when we decide to let God set the agenda in our marriages, not us. When we say, "God, whatever you want from me, I'll do it," rather than, "God, we'd get along so much better if only You would change him," then our marriages will blossom. Instead of getting upset about your differences, see them as opportunities for growth.

I have known many happy marriages, but never a compatible one. The whole aim of marriage is to fight through and survive the instant when incompatibility becomes unquestionable.

G. K. Chesterton, *What's Wrong with the World*

why marriage is so hard

edie wadsworth

You're sitting smack-dab in the middle of the hardest thing in your life—your marriage. How do I know? Because I am too, and I know how the days can seem dark.

You're probably not going to like my answer, but I think I know why being married is so hard. It's not because women are from Venus and men are from Mars. It's not because Scripture is old-fashioned and marriage is passé. I don't even think it's because modern times are so much more volatile to marriage than previous ages, though they may be.

The reason marriage is so hard is because *you're more sinful than you think you are.*

You don't yet grasp the depths of your own depravity. You want your own way. You think your faults are less offensive than his. You justify yourself in a thousand ways and give yourself every benefit of the doubt. But his faults and sins are magnified to you. You're convinced that you give more in the relationship. You are always the hero in your mind. Or maybe not—maybe that's just me.

I've stayed mad for three days because he failed to acknowledge all that I do around here, only to realize that I never once told him thank you for going to work so faithfully all these years—for shouldering the financial responsibility of this gang of kids like a rock. For coming home every single night. For staying when staying seemed so very difficult. Never complaining. Never asking to win an award or be noticed. Just steady and sure and strong.

You are not yet what you ought to be, and so God has been gracious to place you in *this very* relationship, because He means to sanctify you and bring you to repentance. This relationship is hard because it's life and death. What you do here means everything. And you can grumble about the myriad of things that are wrong in this union or you can start to see it how God sees it—as a sacred picture of what He is doing to redeem the world. Christ is the bridegroom and we are the bride. And we will finally be lovely because He has so loved us, not the other way around.

God knew what He was doing when He gave you this particular person. He knew the flaws in your character and personality that this person could sharpen. He knew that this person could expose the sins you try to cover and hide. He knows better than you what you need, and the sooner you submit to Christ and His purposes in your life, the sooner you will see what He is up to in your marriage. This relationship is not for your happiness; it is for your redemption. He is not trying to make you comfortable; He is desperate to make you holy.

He will go to any length to transform you because He loves you so much.

So, what about all my husband's sins, you say? Oh, I know. He is not what he should be either. He has been a failure at being Christ for you. He is selfish and unkind. He's been untrue and weak and childish. He doesn't cherish you the way he should. His love has so seldom been sacrificial.

That's why I'm so glad that my church begins every Sunday morning service with confession and absolution. We stand shoulder to shoulder, he and I, and say what has been so hard to say all week long. And we say it together.

> Most merciful God, we confess that we are by nature sinful and unclean. We have sinned against you in thought, word, and deed, by what we have done and by what we have left undone. We have not loved you with our whole heart and we have not loved our neighbors as ourselves.

I stand there holding the weight of the world—my most grievous sins always against the ones with whom I share the pew. I barely make it through those words most weeks because I know what I am and I know how I fail. This is not some "generic neighbor" I've sinned against. And his sins have torn me apart too. We are faltering and crumbling every day, until these beautiful words restore what we keep trying to tear down.

> Almighty God in His mercy has given His Son to die for you, and for His sake, forgives you all your sins.

God doesn't overlook what you've done. He *sees it all* and yet calls you forgiven and redeemed. Every week—this gift of

195

restoration, healing, and grace astounds us and brings such peace. Words that He paid dearly to speak to us. Words that have the power to do what they say. Words that reach back into the mess we've made of so many strings of days.

In the briefest of moments, I glimpse eternity. I see that this day is not just another block of twenty-four hours but a day that always has been and always will be. Maybe a day marred by my tired rebellion and refusal to give up my ground. Or, just maybe, a day staked with my broken confession and the blessed absolution that comes from knowing He has redeemed every single hour for His glory. This day will come and go and then "day" will be gone. Eternity is breaking through, shouting from beyond—that *all this matters* and that in the end only Love will be left standing, as He holds us both in His glorious Light, darkness falling away around us like a dream.

The best I can ask for is that this love, which has been built on countless failures, will continue to grow. I can say no more than that this is mystery, and gift, and that somehow or other, through grace, our failures can be redeemed and blessed.

Madeleine L'Engle, *The Irrational Season*

writing our love story

You must allow me to tell you how ardently I admire and love you.

Jane Austen, *Pride and Prejudice*

dear husband

laura boggess

Dear Husband,

On the way to school this morning, our youngest, Jeffrey, says to me, "Tell me about your wedding day." The world shifts and I grow lighter and my heart leaps inside of me.

Because thinking of you and the way our love was planted still does that to me.

"Twenty years ago today," I tell him. "The sky was as blue as your eyes. But it was windy. Somewhere there is a picture of Dad holding the skirt of my wedding dress out as it flapped in the wind like a sheet on the clothesline, just waiting for it to settle down so we could take pictures."

And I tell him about that day when we stood before our family and friends and God and made a promise to

199

*love each other forever. And when I return back home
I get out our wedding album.*

Oh, love, how could we have known on this day twenty
years ago all God had planned for us?

"*We got married outside, at the farm,*" *I tell Jeffrey.
"Because Dad and I weren't going to church at the time.
I was still confused about my past. And Dad . . . Dad
did not believe the God-story then.*"

*As I look at our shining faces—twenty years younger—
I think about that.*

Dad did not believe the God-story then.

"*But he does now,*" *Jeffrey responds.*

"*Yes,*" *I say. In June it will be seven years.*

Seven out of twenty years. Thirteen years of prayer.

*What I don't tell Jeffrey is how we almost gave up.
How you told me you didn't think you could be the man
I wanted you to be. How, because of the differences in
the way we believed, you thought maybe it was best to
divorce.*

Remember that, love?

*And isn't the way love endures nothing short of a
miracle? A miracle that takes hard work. And not giving
up. And a whole lot of faith.*

*I look at our shining faces—twenty years younger—
and I see how our love story is really the story of God's
love. The way a marriage shapes a person is the way His
hands mold—making us more beautiful with the lovely
patina of time; conforming us to His image. And I could
say a lot about the bride of Christ and the way marriage*

emulates His love for us and how a man should love his wife the way Christ loves the church.

I could say all those true and beautiful things about our love. After twenty years, and in the looking back, I can see how this story tells the Bigger Story. But I sit here in humble gratitude as I consider the way the pages have unfolded and I feel too tiny to set down words like that.

You have been God's gift to me. He has etched His love into ours.

Later, I will go to the jewelers and pick up my wedding band. I finally had it resized this week. Those few extra pounds and the stretching of this body from carrying our babies made that round gold circle squeeze a little too tight on my finger. Kind of the way it does around my heart. And to me this adding on to the golden promise you gave me seems like a sign of the way love grows too. It can be costly, but in the end it results in more gold.

As God by creation made two of one, so again by marriage He made one of two.

Thomas Adam (attributed)

belated happy valentine's day

rachel anne ridge

I've tried to write about our love story at least half a dozen times. And every time, I've ended up deleting the sappy mess of words and emotion that appears on the screen. There is just no way to cover a lifetime of crazy hard good long deep love in one story, except to say that we are still Valentines.

That guy. Tom asked me to marry him six weeks after our first date. Of course I said yes immediately. He always tells people, "I chased Rachel until she caught me," and it's almost true. I knew right from that first double take that he was going to be the one. Six months after our first date, we were hitched. And what a ride it's been.

Let me tell you about two favorite photos of us.

The first is from when we were engaged: Tom let himself into the UT Arlington stadium in the middle of the night and, armed with a flashlight and a design he'd drawn on grid paper, spelled out "I love you Rachel" in the stands by flipping seats into a pattern. In the morning he took me up in a small plane and flew me over it as he launched into a monologue entitled, "I Wish There Was Some Special Way I Could Tell You How Much I Love You . . . Oh, Look Down There!"

It was epic.

The photo actually appeared in the local paper. Tom landed the plane and we made our way over to the stadium to take pictures, and a photojournalist, who'd seen the gigantic love note from the road, snapped it. What a memory.

Fast-forward twenty-nine years, three kids, two dogs, several cats and gerbils and parakeets, three businesses, some failures, some tough years, and some incredibly awesome times . . . and here we are.

The second photo is from our daughter's wedding in November and I love it because it was such a special moment. We were in the middle of taking family pictures and it just seemed like time went into slow motion and everything was good and beautiful and sweet and perfect. I don't know—we were just a couple of kids who fell crazy in love and made this life with each other and suddenly there we were . . . our kids all grown up and finding their own way and somehow it was coming back to the two of us. I could almost picture every moment of our history—the toddlers, the middle school years, the piano lessons, the braces, the job losses, the health scares, the babies we lost, the graduations, and now the weddings. So much has happened and yet so much has stayed the same. We're still those crazy kids, still laughing at the same corny lines, and still getting angry over the same petty things. I'm still messy and he's still a neat freak. We each still think the other is hot.

203

And we're still Valentines.

In years past, we've made this day about the kids and making sure they felt loved. Sometimes we've even forgotten to celebrate it. But this year we are feeling a little bit giddy again. Maybe it's that life is about to turn another corner and things will once again change when the last of our kids takes off for college. Or maybe it's just that we feel the depth of the life we've forged and the experiences we've shared that have become our story.

There is no Small Thing today, except to celebrate the love in your life—whatever that looks like. In my experience, love is less about flowers and chocolates and more about changing diapers, paying bills, and simply being there for the other person no matter what. Love is long and hard and crazy and good. It's awesome if you get a bouquet of flowers every now and then, but what's even more awesome is when you look across the table at the person you married and know you'd do it all over again. To know that you didn't get the "perfect" life together, you just got a shot at making the "best" life together. And that every day you get a new chance to make it work, to share the load, to dance in the kitchen, and to hold hands on the couch. You get a new chance to love and forgive and overlook and celebrate.

You are making your own love story happen.

Marriage has the power to set the course of your life as a whole. If your marriage is strong, even if all the circumstances in your life around you are filled with trouble and weakness, it won't matter. You will be able to move out into the world in strength.

Tim Keller, *The Meaning of Marriage:*
Facing the Complexities of Commitment
with the Wisdom of God

after all these years

kris camealy

I met you promptly after I swore off boys who didn't love Jesus. I prayed in my car, in the church parking lot, some eighteen years ago—that the next boy I met would not only love Jesus but that he would be *the one*. I think I met you within a week of that day.

We lived fifteen minutes from each other, but it may as well have been two hundred miles. Different sides of town, different high schools. I knew it then, that first day, you towering over all of the other people in the pew. I pronounced our inevitable marriage after one date. But the truth is, I knew it before then. You were the one, the answer to a prayer I barely finished praying before you showed up.

Today we celebrate fourteen years of married living. We've shared one apartment and three houses, two stints in temporary living, a dog, and several fish—remember that time we traveled from Florida to Georgia with a half-full fish tank in the backseat? That was ~~stupid~~ *something*, eh?

Four kids later, here we are. We've traded cars and stomach viruses and colds; we've won (and lost) bets against each other on the Superbowl, year after year. Our bodies have swelled from good living, good eating, and lots of work but not enough working out.

We've lost our cool and countless nights of sleep. We've lost keys, wallets, purses, socks—and occasionally our minds.

We've learned the art of war and how to make peace even when I'm certain I'm right. We've seen forgiveness right up close and felt the warm embrace of redemption—*repeatedly*.

We've seen negative balances in the checking account and we've laughed and cried through movies and the evening news. We've wrestled with life and loss and snuggled in love and clung close in the storms and struggled not to push away in the aftermath.

We've wiped bottoms for eight years and spent too much time and money on diapers and at urgent care. We prayed for one and we got one. We prayed for another and God gave us that one too. Then the girls came right when we asked—really, it is a complete miracle that we have four healthy kids who were formed within days of our asking.

I shake my head at what God's managed to do with us in fourteen years. It's nothing short of a miracle of mercy. You've loved me with the kind of sacrificial love mostly seen in movies that feels too ridiculous to be real—and yet I've lived under that kind of care, with you.

It's been eighteen years since we met. We've seen each other in all varieties of light, for good and otherwise. We've grown up together all these years, and some days I still think it's a wonder we made it through the honeymoon phase—which we can both laughingly agree was *anything* but. We've hit speed bumps and gotten tickets, repaired cars and scraped our knees. We nearly burned down that first apartment on Ponderosa—*oh!* How we howl at that story now.

Our lives are ordinarily extraordinary. We live and love by faith, knowing that our survival depends on something more substantial than a feeling that waxes and wanes with time and circumstance.

Christ has always been the very core of our relationship and who we are as a unit. We are *one* made from three, and He is our very center. When we lose our way and our vision, when we forget which side we're on, we find the answers in Him. He draws us in and holds us steady.

It's only been fourteen years, sharing a bed and a bathroom and a closet. We've only enjoyed daily meals together at the same table for *just* fourteen years. It sounds so young.

There is (Lord willing) much more time to spend together.

This is what a marriage looks like—a mix of grime and glory. A mad swirling of *losts* and *founds*. Christ is who and *how* we cling, when the world bears down outside our door.

After all of these years, we find ourselves still dancing this same dance, but better.

So much better than when the music first started.

"For I know the plans I have for you," declares the LORD, "plans to prosper you and not to harm you, plans to give you hope and a future."

Jeremiah 29:11 NIV

shirtless nostalgia

mandy arioto

Fifteen years ago I went for a run along the beach in San Diego, accompanied by my roommate. We laced up our running shoes and set out for a Saturday morning jog. We were in college, and what else do you have to do when you're twenty-one other than spend a leisurely Saturday morning breathing in salt air and enjoying the ten a.m. sunshine? A few miles into our run brought us to a place on the beach where the path ran parallel to a forty-foot cliff with no railing. As we jogged along this treacherous piece of coast I noticed a guy running toward us. He was wearing a pair of running shorts, no shirt, and was totally hot. He got closer and I recognized him. He attended the same college as I did, and though we hadn't met I had seen him around campus. As we ran closer I tried to play it cool, pick up the pace, and not look like I was sweating too much. And then, just as we got close enough to make eye contact, he tripped right in front of me, letting out an "Ugh!" and almost falling down the forty-foot cliff. He quickly regained his composure—and his footing—and kept running without saying another word. My friend and I kept running too, and as soon as we were out of his hearing range she looked at me and said, "He totally has a crush on you."

Fast-forward a week and I get a message on my phone from the "shirtless wonder." He tracked down my phone number and utilized his most impressive verbal skills to convince me to go on a date with him. The rest, as they say, is history. To be honest, Joe had me from the moment I saw him shirtless and teetering on the edge of the cliff.

This past week we went to San Diego for Thanksgiving. While we were there, Joe and I went on a date to the spot he first fell for me. We ran on the beach, reminiscing about our whirlwind romance and the three whirlwind children that are the by-products of that romance. We talked feelings and hopes and remembered all of the silly things we did in the early stages of our relationship. Most of all, we remembered what started this whole thing in the first place.

I can't tell you that the last fifteen years have been easy. We have endured hard times where all we were running on were the fumes from the romance that drew us together in the first place. There have been financial struggles and moments when I wondered if we were ever going to have fun together again. The weight of life stacks up sometimes. It is in those moments that nostalgia saves us. Remembering the spark that kindled a lifetime of commitment can reignite that fire a second time.

I wouldn't trade any of the adventures we have had since that first fateful meeting on the cliffs. And I am the luckiest girl in the world that the man of my dreams literally fell into my life (and shirtless nonetheless).

Friendship is a deep oneness that develops when two people, speaking the truth in love to one another, journey together to the same horizon.

Tim Keller, *The Meaning of Marriage: Facing the Complexities of Commitment with the Wisdom of God*

the security of our story

renee swope

Carrying plates to the table, mashed potatoes and gravy piled high, I watch as my teenage boys plop down in their chairs. Peeling black paint reveals my secret—the original white enamel. I smile, remembering this was the first piece of furniture their dad and I bought together.

We've sat around this table sharing stories and meals with these two boys for almost two decades. Tonight we'll sit and talk and linger longer. No homework to finish or friends to meet. Cell phones and emails won't distract us. Their five-year-old sister won't interrupt us. Although she would love to be part of our special occasion, she isn't fond of sitting still. So tonight it's just us four.

We'll have dinner and dessert, and our favorite flavored coffee, as we celebrate our twenty-year wedding anniversary. I want to reminisce about the details of our story. I want to tell our boys how we met. How I knew their dad was the one

I wanted to marry. How I knew he was the man *God* wanted me to marry.

I've scripted the scene and the dialogue. I know there will be eye rolls and resistance, but I also know they will *remember* this. And I want them to remember. This. Our story. Their story.

Much to my surprise, both Joshua and Andrew start asking questions. They want to hear more about the time we planned a hiking trip with friends, when we were "just" friends, and no one else showed up except us two. They ask about the first year we were married and why we couldn't afford cable TV. *They want to hear our story.* And I am surprised.

Reminiscing about how we met and why we decided to get married seemed like just a fun way to celebrate . . . but I think it goes deeper. Our love story tells our children that we are not only husband and wife but also friends. Our love story gives our kids assurance that we really love each other and are committed to staying together—no matter what.

Our love story helps our children see their beginning while adding laughter and security to their everyday in-betweens. And even if ours isn't the happily-ever-after story we hoped for, it still has meaning in our children's lives.

As a teenager, I asked my mom, more than once, to tell me how she and Dad met and why she liked him. Although their love story ended in divorce before I was two years old, hearing their story always made me feel like I was meant to be. I wonder if that's why my teenage boys leaned in and listened.

Hearing our love story gives our children the assurance that they were meant to be. After all, without that first date, there would be none of the wonder that followed—the love, the wedding, the dog, the kids, the memories. All because their mom and dad fell in love.

Your eyes saw my unformed body;
    all the days ordained for me were written in
      your book
    before one of them came to be.

Psalm 139:16 NIV

what i want my daughters
to know about my wedding

kristen welch

Dear daughters,

A few months ago you were both in a wedding, and between that and all the popular TLC bridal shows on Netflix and the breathtaking wedding boards on Pinterest, it's got you asking questions about my wedding.

So, I want to tell you about it. First of all, it was ugly. No, really, it was. It was 1994, so that didn't help. Neither did my temporary romantic love for the Victorian era. My accent colors were mauve and forest green. Yeah. They were interesting colors against the burnt orange pews of the church and twinkling Christmas trees on the stage. (It was a December wedding.) The bridesmaids wore handmade, mauve, tentlike dresses that could accommodate an array of sizes, including a very pregnant bridesmaid. I'm pretty sure they were burned while I was on my honeymoon.

I had always planned on wearing a long-sleeved ivory Victorian gown. But instead I fell in love with a white off-the-shoulder sequined contemporary one. I had multiple themes going on. Remember when you found my dress in a box in the attic a couple of years ago and asked if you could try it on? That kind of stuff is hard on moms.

The reception was in the small, dimly lit fellowship hall. There wasn't dinner or dancing or enough satin to cover the drabness of the room. There was some sort of Sprite punch, a delicious wedding cake, a groom's cake (with a plastic fisherman on top), and some mixed nuts.

There weren't party favors or sparklers. The guests threw birdseed as we ran to my blue Isuzu compact car, awash with ridiculous writing and a condom on the muffler (your uncle's contribution). I can still remember the look on the pastor's face as we waved good-bye.

We immediately stopped at a fast-food restaurant, where I dumped a pint of birdseed from my underwear onto the floor of the bathroom. That was wrong. But it was itchy.

I can't think of a single pin-worthy picture from the day. It wasn't trendy or lavish. There wasn't a dance floor or fresh orchids or chandeliers hanging from trees. But I wouldn't change a moment of it.

Somehow even with our less than glamorous wedding photo album and our honeymoon on an extreme

217

budget to exotic Arkansas, your dad and I will celebrate twenty years of marriage this Christmas.

Because we understood that a marriage isn't about a wedding. We discovered that a lifetime of love and commitment trumps an event any day. We learned that starting our new life together debt- and doubt-free was a gift to each other.

Yesterday, I read that 70 percent of girls creating wedding boards on Pinterest aren't even engaged yet. With every other marriage ending, do we have time for all this planning and pining for one perfect day?

It makes me sad that the world you're growing up in concentrates more on the wedding than the marriage. It's over in a sunset and it's easy compared to the long marathon of becoming and staying one with your one and only.

I want you to know marriage is more than a venue or a menu. It's far more than The Perfect Day or saying yes to the dress. And I know you will probably want all of the above someday. And that's okay.

I just want you to spend more time praying than planning. I want you to sacrifice more than you spend. I want you to understand your commitment to the man of your dreams is more than a certificate—it's a covenant with God.

Most of all, I want you to know love. The kind of love your dad and I have, that lasts through heartache and headaches. I want you to know that you are loved. You don't have to earn or achieve it. It's not dependent on a good hair day or bad. It's not something you can *lose. Whether you're swept off your feet or remain a confident single woman, you are enough.*

I have seen how fast time flies. I know the days are long and the years are short. I put away the toys and clothes you outgrow regularly. I know while I write this one of you is practicing eye shadow upstairs and the other is practicing cartwheels in the yard, and I will blink and it will be time to give you away.

You are just beginning to dream. Don't stop.

And on this regular day, I want you to know that my wedding wasn't much.

But my marriage is more.

Love,
Mom

For where your treasure is, there will your heart be also.

Matthew 6:21

the secret to a happy marriage

shawn smucker

Can it really have taken me
sixteen years to realize you can
live in the same house with someone
and still lose track of them?

It's true.

We occasionally lose
each other somewhere among
discarded LEGOs and Everest piles
of laundry, too many words to be written,
or deciding the best way to teach
dangling participles.
Our words
cross and mismatch and fall,
seeds on parched August ground, hard
as pavement. Is

there a more complicated maze

than the everyday household routine?
Is there anywhere easier to lose someone
than in the daily humdrum of a life?

The two of us
we go from found to lost
in the time it takes to zombie-walk
to the baby's bed at 2 am and fall
asleep on the scratchy carpet, in the time
it takes to nurse a child's hurt feelings on
the third floor, coming back to bed
only to find the
other has already fallen asleep.

Maybe the key to this thing called
marriage
isn't remaining in love
(Lord knows I love you)
or sticking to those vows
(rules parch and crack and can't
keep a meaningful thing together)
but maybe
the key is finding the energy
the courage
to keep finding each other again
and again.

They leave us after dinner, all
five children, and we're staring
the vast distance from one end of the table
to the other, because a family this size
requires a large table, and the distance
from one end to the other

can feel like the span of the Sahara. Lost
and found.

But then one of us moves closer
and we talk quietly while the sound
of their steps rains down from above.
Or we walk this city in which I love you,
holding hands
breathing in the lights
remembering the sweet feeling
that casual ecstasy
of being found again
by someone you have loved for so long.

Maybe the key to finding each other
is discovering ways
every day
that we can get lost
together
all over again. Maybe the seeds
that fall on pavement can still
find the winding crack
burrow deep
and sprout green life
in this city.

You have been in every line I have ever read.

Charles Dickens, *Great Expectations*

with this ring

{part 3}

dawn camp

We moved from Arkansas to Atlanta with one car, a fourteen-month-old baby, and a U-Haul containing all our worldly possessions. We passed through Memphis on the tenth anniversary of Elvis's death, a date I use to calculate when we moved to Atlanta, and spent the night at a dirty motel in Dalton, the carpet capital of Georgia. We needed sleep before those final ninety miles when we would drive a trailer on I-285.

We lived lean, as newlyweds often do. I counted pennies and measured any amount of money we spent by how many McDonald's cheeseburgers it would buy. When we needed a car, my daddy loaned us the blue '73 Mustang convertible I had driven in high school. I remember driving down Buford

223

Highway with the top down and the radio blaring "The Way You Make Me Feel," the sun warm on my face.

We moved to the suburbs, I graduated from Emory University with a degree in Russian, and we had a second son. Over the years our family continued to grow, and now we have four boys and four girls, our own version of the Brady Bunch. I know the answer to the questions: same husband, no twins, on purpose.

We bought our first freestanding home (we'd owned a duplex once, years earlier) from my parents and moved our family of six there. Our fifth child and second daughter arrived in December 1999, just two weeks before the dreaded Y2K problem, which thankfully was more bark than bite. Our house sat on a hill with a wooded backyard and a screened room off the back deck. Trees came almost right up to the house and we used a field guide to identify the birds in their limbs. Our favorite was the indigo bunting, robed in a glorious shade of blue. My father-in-law and my husband built a two-level treehouse—a housewarming gift from my in-laws—in the middle of the yard, a cozy, private spot for school or lunch or settling down with a good book. It's the thing I miss most about that home.

Bryan continued to wear the gold nugget ring that replaced his lost wedding ring, but with time it wore down until it actually separated in the back. We had no idea what a blessing that small gap would be!

Our garage door was a cantankerous thing. One day Bryan, a frequent and successful DIYer, replaced a couple of its panels and then attempted to tighten the coil at the top of the door when he finished. Now I know it's called a torsion spring.

Now I know how dangerous they are to work on because the springs are under such tension. Now I know experienced professional installers wind up in the emergency room with injuries from working on them. But then I knew nothing; I didn't even know to be afraid. As Bryan used the tool to tighten the spring, it suddenly uncoiled, caught his ring, and shot it across the garage. We found it there, curved like a horseshoe. Without that gap in the band, he surely would have lost his finger. The ring caught the inside of his pinky as it was torn from his hand; he wears a scar there as a reminder of what might have been.

Over the years my parents, sister, cousins, aunt, great-aunts, and grandmother made their way to Georgia too. My grandmother and two never-married great-aunts, nicknamed the Golden Girls, lived in a rental house close to ours. We visited them shortly after our garage door experience, and as we climbed back in our car, my grandmother followed us outside, slow and unsteady as she was, and approached Bryan's window. In her outstretched hand she held my beloved granddad's ring. Years later I can't write these words without tears in my eyes. What she offered as a replacement means more to me than the original ring I put on Bryan's finger not long after our wedding day. Seeing Granddad's ring on my husband's finger makes me so happy.

On our twenty-fifth anniversary Bryan took a knee, just like when he proposed, and held out a ring worn by both my mother and grandmother (who had a tendency to lose rings; I'm not sure how many my granddad bought her). After my mother passed away, my sister kept her original wedding ring (worn during our childhood) and I kept this one, which she wore in later years. If I wanted to wear that ring and the history it represented, Bryan offered it now. For a while I alternated rings, but now my hands tend to swell and I wear the new set—actually the older set—all the time, so my hand holds a piece of family history too.

Before his wedding day one of our sons asked if there were any other rings in the family. And his bride slipped my daddy's ring—the one he wore when my mother was alive (I have a stepmom now and he wears her ring)—on his finger when they spoke their vows. I would love to look into the future and see where our rings will travel and what hands they'll grace, how they'll contribute to stories yet to be penned. But today I'm thankful my children and grandchildren will know our story, the history of these rings we wear.

contributors

Mandy Arioto is the president and CEO of MOPS International and lives with her family in Denver, Colorado. Her new book *Starry Eyed: Seeing Grace in the Unfolding Constellations of Life and Motherhood* released in August 2016. See what she is up to at mandyjarioto.com.

Diane Bailey is a freelance writer and founder of The Consilium—a community of wisdom and purpose. She encourages women with humor and biblical principles about stepfamilies, finding purpose after the nest is empty, and leadership. She blogs about her perfectly imperfect life at dianewbailey.net.

Lisa-Jo Baker is the author of *Surprised by Motherhood: Everything I Never Expected about Being a Mom* and the community manager for *(in)courage*. Her writings on motherhood are syndicated from New Zealand to New York, and you can catch up with her daily chaos at lisajobaker.com.

Gregory Bledsoe, MD, MPH, is a board certified emergency medicine physician who currently serves as the Surgeon General for the state of Arkansas. Dr. Bledsoe is a frequent guest writer and public speaker, and the chief editor of the medical text *Expedition and Wilderness Medicine* published by Cambridge University Press. He lives in Little Rock, Arkansas, with his wife and three daughters.

Laura Boggess is the author of *Playdates with God: Having a Childlike Faith in a Grown-up World*. She blogs at lauraboggess.com, where she shares stories about chasing after the blue flower. Laura spends her days working as a counselor in a medical rehabilitation hospital and her evenings doing laundry. She lives in a little valley in West Virginia with her husband and their two teenage sons, who make a lot of dirty laundry.

Kris Camealy is a writer and teacher in middle Ohio. She spends her days homeschooling her four kids and working on her next book. She is the founder of GraceTable.org, a hospitality-themed website. Kris tells redemption stories at kriscamealy.com.

Dawn Camp is an Atlanta-based writer, wife, mother of eight, and editor and photographer of *The Beauty of Grace* and *The Gift of Friendship*. She lives with a camera in one hand and a glass of sweet tea in the other, and blogs family, faith, and Photoshop at myhomesweethomeonline.net and also contributes to incourage.me.

Mary Carver is a writer, speaker, wife, mom—and recovering perfectionist. She lives for good books, spicy queso, and television marathons, but she lives because of God's grace. Mary writes about her imperfect life with humor and honesty at givinguponperfect.com. She is also the coauthor of *Choose Joy: Finding Hope & Purpose When Life Hurts*.

Robin Dance, married to her college sweetheart and mom to three, dreams of Neverland and Narnia. She's a ragamuffin princess and as Southern as sugar-shocked tea. She's sometimes lost, sometimes found, and always celebrates redemptive purpose at robindance.me.

Richard Paul Evans is the #1 *New York Times* and *USA Today* bestselling author of more than twenty-five novels, including *The Christmas Box* and Michael Vey, an award-winning young adult series. Richard is the founder and chairman of The Christmas Box International, an organization that provides shelter and care for abused and neglected children. Richard lives in Salt Lake City with his wife, Keri, and their five children.

Shaunti Feldhahn is a wife and mom first and a popular speaker and bestselling author second. After receiving a graduate degree from Harvard, Shaunti started out on Wall Street and today investigates life-changing truths about relationships, published in globally popular books such as *For Women Only* and *For Parents Only*.

Joy Forney is the wife of a missionary pilot and momma to five. Living abroad brings her to the foot of the cross time and time again, and no matter her geographical location, she still finds Him faithful. She blogs about her adventure of a life at joyforney.org.

Holley Gerth is a bestselling author of books like *You're Already Amazing*, a life coach, and a speaker. She also cofounded the website incourage.me and blogs at holleygerth.com.

Sheila Wray Gregoire is a Christian speaker, columnist, and author. She's written five books, including *The Good Girl's Guide to Great Sex*. She loves speaking about marriage, parenting, and keeping our eyes on Jesus. She lives in Ontario, Canada, with her husband of over twenty years; together they have two grown daughters.

Mo Isom is a professional author and speaker. She was an All-American goalkeeper for the LSU soccer team and the first female to try out for an SEC men's football team. She lives with her husband and daughter in Atlanta, where she facilitates a faith-centered blog at moisom.com.

Lisa Jacobson and her husband, Matthew, enjoy raising and home-educating their eight children in the beautiful Pacific Northwest. She shares her passion for husband, home, and family at her popular blog club31women.com. She's also the author of *100 Ways to Love Your Husband*.

Alia Joy Hagenbach is a storyteller, speaker, and homeschooling mother of three. She shares her story in broken bits and pieces on her blog aliajoy.com and finds community where other's stories intersect. She's also a regular contributor at *Grace Table*, *SheLoves*, and *(in)courage*.

Alexandra Kuykendall is the author of *The Artist's Daughter: A Memoir* and *Loving My Actual Life: An Experiment in*

Relishing What's Right in Front of Me. She lives in Denver with her husband, Derek, and their four daughters. Connect with her at alexandrakuykendall.com.

Kelley J. Leigh is a midlife writer and a mom to four sons. Kelley lives in a quirky little mountain town in Colorado, where she writes openly about intimacy issues and recovery in marriage and faith. Find her over at kelleyjleigh.com.

Shannon Lowe blogged for many years at rocksinmydryer .typepad.com. Her writing has appeared in numerous books and magazines, including *Good Housekeeping*, *Parenting*, and *Chicken Soup for the New Mom's Soul*. She lives in Oklahoma with her husband and four kids.

Shannan Martin is a speaker and writer who found her voice in the country and her story in the city. She and her jail-chaplain husband, Cory, have four funny children who came to them across oceans and rivers. Having sold their dream farmhouse, they now live in Goshen, Indiana. She writes the popular blog *Flower Patch Farmgirl*. Her first book, *Falling Free: Rescued from the Life I Always Wanted*, released in September 2016.

Shelly Miller is a veteran ministry leader and sought-after mentor on Sabbath-keeping. She leads the Sabbath Society, an online community of people who want to make rest a rhythm of life, and her writing has been featured in several national publications. She is the author of *Rhythms of Rest: Finding the Spirit of Sabbath in a Busy World* (Bethany, October 2016). Visit Shelly's blog, *Redemption's Beauty*, for stories

231

about the adventure of living as an expat in London. She is a vicar's wife and mother of two children.

Erin Mohring is a freelance writer and speaker who shares about her faith, family, fitness, and fashion at homewiththe boys.net. She is the cofounder of Raising Boys Ministries and themobsociety.com. Erin lives with her husband and three sons in Nebraska, where she enjoys running, reading, and eating popcorn.

Lynn D. Morrissey is the author of *Love Letters to God: Deeper Intimacy through Written Prayer* and other books, contributor to numerous bestsellers, Consilium blogger, speaker, and soloist. A professional journal facilitator (CJF), she's passionate about encouraging transparency in women through her ministry, Sacred Journaling. She and Michael have been married since 1975 and have one beautiful grown daughter, Sheridan. Contact her at words@brick.net or on Facebook.

Angela Nazworth is passionate about living life with a heart wide open. She writes mostly about the beauty of grace, friendship, vulnerability, and community for incourage.me and on her personal blog, angelanazworth.com.

Crystal Paine is a wife, mom of three, founder of moneysaving mom.com, and author of the *New York Times* bestseller *Say Goodbye to Survival Mode*.

Laura Parker, having lived in four countries with her family, now calls Thailand home. She and her husband lead a nonprofit organization called The Exodus Road, which fights sex trafficking. She has published a book about their journey entitled *The Exodus Road* and blogs at lauraparkerwrites .com.

Rachel Anne Ridge is an artist and writer, mom to three grown kids, and Nana to two littles. She blogs daily humor and encouragement at homesanctuary.com. Her first book, *Flash, The Donkey*, released in May 2015 (Tyndale).

Deidra Riggs is a national speaker and writer who works to build bridges and tear down the walls that divide us—in our culture, our neighborhoods, our hearts, and the church. Engage in the conversation with Deidra and her community at her website, deidrariggs.com, each month at incourage .me, @deidrariggs on Instagram (her favorite) and Twitter, or follow her on Facebook. Deidra is the author of *Every Little Thing: Making a World of Difference Right Where You Are.*

Liz Sagaser writes and edits full-time for MOPS International (mops.org). She and her husband raise two kids, a cat, a puppy, and a salamander in the Black Hills of South Dakota. In her spare time she coaches writers and businesses on becoming better communicators. Connect with her at liz .sagaser@gmail.com.

Ashleigh Slater is the author of *Team Us: Marriage Together*. She spends her time drinking coffee, hanging out with her four daughters, and binge-watching TV shows with her husband, Ted. To learn more about Ashleigh, visit ashleighslater .com.

Shawn Smucker is the author of the young adult novel *The Day the Angels Fell* as well as numerous nonfiction books including *Building a Life Out of Words* and *How to Use a Runaway Truck Ramp*. He lives in the city of Lancaster, Pennsylvania, with his wife and their six children.

Marci Stevens is a wife, mother, speaker, and blogger. She is also cofounder of a powerful nonprofit, award-winning marriage ministry, Marriage Pressure Points. Marci writes about her own weaknesses as a wife in hopes that God will redeem all of her messes.

Crystal Stine is passionate about living authentically, chasing joy, and encouraging women to savor the season God has them in. She works full-time as the editorial and marketing manager at *(in)courage* and shares daily encouragement at her blog, crystalstine.me.

Ann Swindell is an author, speaker, and teacher who is passionate about seeing women set free by the love of Jesus. She writes for various publications and her first book, a memoir called *Still Waiting*, will release in 2017. After teaching college courses for years, Ann now offers online writing courses to help others strengthen and sharpen their writing voice, ability, and craft at writingwithgrace.com. You can connect with Ann online at annswindell.com or @annswindell.

Renee Swope is a Word-lover, heart-encourager, storyteller, and grace-needer. Through her written and spoken words, Renee empowers with courage and equips others with confidence to make a difference right where they are, with what they already have! She is a speaker, radio cohost, and best-selling author of *A Confident Heart* and *A Confident Heart Devotional*. Connect with Renee online at reneeswope.com, monthly at incourage.me, @reneeswope on Instagram and Twitter, or in her Facebook communities: facebook.com /aconfidentheart and facebook.com/reneeswope.

Edie Wadsworth is a momma, writer, blogger, foodie, cowboy boot–wearer, and hospitality fiend. She's a lover of truth, beauty, and goodness and seeks to inspire women in their love and service of others at the lifestyle blog lifeingrace blog.com. Her memoir, *All the Pretty Things*, released in September 2016.

Kristen Welch is a blogger (wearethatfamily.com) and the author of *Raising Grateful Kids in an Entitled World: How One Family Learned That Saying No Can Lead to Life's Biggest Yes* (Tyndale, 2016) and *Rhinestone Jesus: Saying Yes to God When Sparkly Safe Faith Is No Longer Enough* (Tyndale, 2014). In 2010 she and her family founded a nonprofit, Mercy House Kenya, that empowers pregnant mothers living in extreme poverty with opportunity. Between writing and saying yes to God, Kristen enjoys life in Texas with her best friend and three awesome kids.

Emily T. Wierenga is an award-winning journalist, artist, and the author of six books including her first novel, *A Promise in Pieces* (2014), her memoir, *Atlas Girl: Finding Home in the Last Place I Thought to Look* (Baker, 2014) and its sequel, *Making It Home* (Baker, 2015). In June 2014 she founded The Lulu Tree, a nonprofit dedicated to preventing tomorrow's orphans by equipping today's mothers in the slum of Katwe, Uganda.

Francie Winslow lives in the Washington, DC, area with her husband and four kids. As a speaker and writer, Francie's passion is to see women and families discipled and made whole in Christ. Find her at franciewinslow.com.

Get to know

Dawn Camp

Read her blog

&

Join the conversation

MyHomeSweetHomeOnline.net

"*This compilation* of memoirs and personal stories written by a group of leading female Christian authors, including Ann Voskamp, Tsh Oxereider, and Holley Gerth, points readers toward Christ."

—*Life:Beautiful* magazine

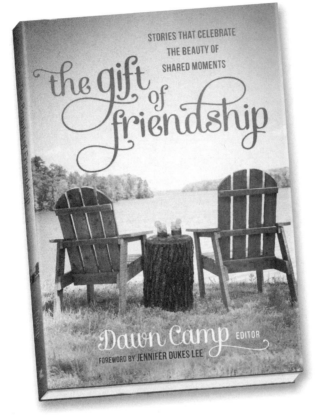